THE MENTOR QUEST

The Mentor Quest

Practical Ways to Find the Guidance You Need

BETTY SOUTHARD

SERVANT PUBLICATIONS
ANN ARBOR, MICHIGAN

Vine Books is an imprint of Servant Publications especially designed to serve evangelical Christians.

Scripture verses marked NIV are from the New International Version. Verses marked LB are from the Living Bible. Verses marked NKJV and KJV are from the New King James Version and the King James Version respectively. Verses marked RSV are from the Revised Standard Version.

To protect the privacy of some of the individuals whose stories are told in this book, names and characterizations have been fictionalized, although they are based on real events. With permission, real names and events are portrayed in most of the stories.

Published by Servant Publications
P.O. Box 8617
Ann Arbor, Michigan 48107

Cover design by Alan Furst, Minneapolis, Minn.

02 03 04 05 10 9 8 7 6 5 4 3 2 1

Printed in the United States of America
ISBN 1-56955-309-2

Library of Congress Cataloging-in-Publication Data

Southard, Betty.
    The mentor quest : practical ways to find the guidance you need /
Betty Southard.
        p. cm.
    ISBN 1-56955-309-2 (alk. paper)
    1. Mentoring in church work. I. Title.
    BV4408.5 .S68 2002
    253' .7—dc21

                                                            2001006402

Dedication

To my husband, Fred,
whose encouragement, inspiration,
and constant belief in me,
along with his willingness to fend for himself
while I am immersed in writing,
free me to be all that I am.

Contents

Acknowledgments

Special thanks to Marita Littauer for her mentoring in so many areas. I am also grateful for the prayers and encouragement of my writers' focus group: Armené, Pat, Ann, Vicki, Georgia, and Gayle, and for my prayer partner, Jan Stoop. Thanks, too, to my parents and the wonderful heritage and example their lives have been.

I am particularly grateful to Catherine Marshall, Corrie ten boom, Mother Teresa, Lillian Dickson, Richard Foster, and Florence Littauer, whose wisdom, insights, and struggles shared through writing and speaking have mentored me through the years.

CHAPTER ONE

Who Will Mentor Me?

I will never forget my first and only meeting with Lillian Dickson. The year was 1973, and we were on a tour with our pastor and his wife. Lillian was a small woman, not particularly attractive. Her face was weather-beaten and her clothing out of style. Her voice was rather high pitched, and she appeared old. She blew into the lobby of our hotel that Sunday morning, looking rather out of place. It didn't take us long to determine why this woman had the nickname "Typhoon Lil."

"Where is your pastor? Are you ready to go?" she asked, glancing around the lobby and then looking down at her watch. We had an appointment to meet with her at 8:30. We were to be taken to several of the schools, churches, and homes that her organization had built and sponsored.

"We are ready, but our pastor and his wife aren't yet," I replied.

"Well, then, we shall go. I will leave a driver and another car to bring them when they are ready," she said.

And off we went to see the many ministries that Mustard Seed Missions had built in Taipei, on the island of Taiwan. Our first stop was at the home for delinquent boys, those who had been picked up off the streets, often for stealing food to keep them alive. They ranged in age from five to fifteen, and if not for the Mustard Seed Boys' Home would have been in prison or living on the streets. Then we traveled on to the children's home, where young orphans, or children from families who just couldn't support them, were given food, lodging, schooling, and loving care. The rooms were brightly painted and the children's faces full of joy. Their beautiful singing filled our hearts and lifted our spirits.

Next we visited the leprosarium, attending their church service and marveling at the peace and joy reflected on the faces of those who had been so terribly, physically scarred with this disease. After church we toured the facilities and saw the many different training programs that had been implemented to give dignity and a means of support to the men and women living there.

We saw only a fraction of the work that Lillian Dickson had founded in Taipei, for her work covered the island of Taiwan and has spread to Indonesia, Papua New Guinea, and many places in the South Seas. Our visit with Lillian ended in her offices, where she showed us a basket full of requests from communities and governments, asking her to set up schools, hospitals, training centers, and orphanages in their countries. We were overwhelmed and asked what she planned to do with all these requests.

"When God supplies the funds we will meet the needs. I can't take on the whole world, but God can," she replied.

I would love to stay here and shadow this woman as she goes about her mission, I thought. She is my kind of lady. I loved the pace at which she worked. Quick actions and decisions and an ability to size up needs and decipher how best to meet them epitomized her work. She had a passion for making a difference.

Her husband was president of a seminary in Taipei, commissioned as a missionary in his denomination, but that denomination didn't commission the wives as missionaries. When Lil found work that needed to be done and sought mission funds, the red tape and slow response in the face of immediate need propelled her to go directly to God to meet the needs.

Though my personal interaction with Lillian Dickson was limited to that one Sunday so long ago, I consider her one of my mentors. How can that be? Doesn't mentoring require a long-term, personal relationship? Not necessarily.

Lillian modeled for me, through her actions that morning, the difference a single person can make if he or she is willing to look to God for provision and invest his or her energy solely in making things happen. I followed her life and missions through her monthly newsletters, which were filled with enthusiastic reports of the opportunities and challenges that came her way. Never did she beg for money. Her letters were filled with poems and prose and were a ministry to me. She taught me from her experiences to never give up. I learned what raw faith looked like in the most difficult circumstances. I looked forward to those newsletters, which encouraged and challenged me to dream big dreams for God. Lillian continued her work and personally wrote the newsletters until her death in 1983 at the age of eighty-two. Yes, Lillian Dickson was a mentor to me.

Mentoring: A Traditional View

Mentors! What are they? Who needs one? What do they do? How can I find one? Mentors or coaches are the buzzword in today's society, in both the business and the personal arenas. People are looking for ways to improve their skills, expand their influence, and develop their growth potential, and mentoring is increasingly being seen as an effective means to that end.

Mentoring is not a new concept by any means. In fact, we can go back as far as Homer to find the first mentor. In his epic poem *The Odyssey*, Mentor is the name of the male guardian and tutor of Odysseus' son Telemachus. While Odysseus is away fighting at Troy, Mentor raises and teaches Telemachus. Interestingly enough, however, while Mentor is the personal, relational figure in the poem, Athena, mythical goddess of wisdom and the arts, sometimes assumes the "mentoring" role in Telemachus' life. Athena's involvement with Telemachus moves the mentoring experience, in its earliest conception, beyond dependence on a personal relationship with the mentor.

Many books have been written on the topic of mentoring. Most focus only on the relational aspect of mentoring: that of the character of the mentor and his or her function. In their book, *As Iron Sharpens Iron*, Howard and William Hendricks give several definitions of a mentor. They quote Paul Stanley and Robert Clinton (*Connecting*) as saying: "Mentoring is a relational process in which a mentor, who knows or has experienced something ... transfers that something to a mentee, at an appropriate time and manner, so that it facilitates development or empowerment."

Linda Phillips-Jones (*The New Mentors* and *Protégés*), also quoted by Hendricks, says, "In modern-day terms, mentors are influential, experienced people who *personally* (italics mine) help you reach your major life goals."

Bobb Biehl said, in a 1993 Promise Keepers Workshop, "Defining mentoring is sort of tough, but describing it is pretty easy. It's like having an uncle that cares for you for a lifetime, and wants to see you do well."[1]

All of these definitions depend on a long-term personal relationship with a particular person who will assume the responsibility of teacher, advisor, sponsor, and more.

Yet is that the only way mentoring can occur?

The Myths of Mentoring

Many misconceptions surround the concept of mentoring, often clouding perceptions of its usefulness. Some believe a person must have just one mentor for life, or that a mentor must be an "older" person. Others believe that mentors must have special training, education, and skills, plus a commitment to making change happen in another. This is particularly true in the new arena of mentoring often called coaching. Unfortunately, with all the recent emphasis on the importance of having a mentor or a personal coach, many people believe that their inability to find a mentor for themselves precludes them from becoming all they were meant to be.

Even the title "mentor" or "mentee" often scares away a potential mentor or seeker. It implies lessons, structure, discipline, accountability, and maybe, most discouraging, time. In an age of "instants" we don't really want to spend a lot of time working at growth. We want quick and easy answers, a self-applied "Miracle-Gro."

Some have found a "mentor" only to be disappointed in the relationship when it did not live up to their expectations. Often there is confusion on the part of both participants as to the goals and reasons for the relationship. Part of that confusion comes from the varying descriptions of mentors that are found in the many books on the subject.

Most of the books on mentoring are designed to equip men and women to use their age and experience to become a mentor. There are also a few books on the market meant to help eager future mentees find the right mentor for their needs. While all of this literature is helpful in learning how to mentor and be mentored through an ongoing personal relationship, there is little in these books to encourage those of us who, for one reason or another, have not found "our mentor."

Perhaps the reason why so many of us have not discovered our mentors, is that we don't understand exactly what mentoring means. Perhaps we first need to take another look at the mentoring process.

Personal Evaluation

1. How have you experienced God's direction in your life?
2. What is your definition of mentoring?

CHAPTER TWO

Mentoring: A New Look

Focus on the Family recently aired a radio program on mentoring. As I listened, the hunger within me for a special someone to mentor me was stirred once again. I thought of the many times I had heard the glowing testimonies of people who had found that one special person whose counsel and wisdom had guided their path through the years. Yet, I had never experienced the type of mentoring of which they spoke. As I thought about it, I realized that indeed, I had been mentored, just not in the traditional way.

Mentoring is a process of linking people to the resources of others, empowering them for greater personal growth and effectiveness. Leonard Sweet says, "the role of the Christian mentor is that of a lamp to illumine the pathway that lies directly at his or her student's feet, offering guidance and service in indirect ways."[1]

I have discovered many "mentors" according to Sweet's definition, who, like Typhoon Lil, have illumined my pathway, but none of them have been in the context of formal mentoring relationships. That hasn't kept me from being mentored, though. I want to help you discover ways that you, too, can be "mentored" outside of the conventional method of mentoring. Let me share with you my personal experience.

Throughout my years of teaching, speaking, and writing, many people have approached me seeking the secrets of balanced living. I find that people everywhere are hungry to fill the aching inner void in their lives. Many have asked, "Will you be my mentor?" After I had heard this questions dozens of times, I began to ask myself, "How have I arrived at the place in life where others see in me what I have been so desperately looking for in others? That is, how did I become mentor material without having had a mentor myself?"

As I began to trace my growth I discovered that I was indeed "mentored" through the years, even though it was never in the traditional sense. I was linked to the resources of others in many ways. Sometimes the mentoring was formal; more often it was informal. Occasionally it was scheduled; but more often it was sporadic. The exchanging of resources sometimes took place over a long period of time; yet sometimes it occurred in a one-time encounter. Such empowerment might happen face-to-face, but it might also happen over a great distance. Sometimes the exchange was personal, one-on-one, yet at other times I encountered it as a member of an audience or a participant in a discussion. I have discovered many new thoughts and ideas through reading, answering questions, and hearing the comments of others.

Surrounded at an Early Age

I have always had a deep hunger for growth, particularly spiritual growth. Though I have never had a formal mentoring arrangement, that has not kept me from learning from others whatever and whenever possible. It started at a very young age as I observed the men and women in my local church congregation. I listened to their words, watched the way they conducted themselves, and noted the interactions of their families.

I grew up in the Quaker (Evangelical Friends) denomination, in a small congregation, where it was common to have personal testimonies during the church services. Each service had a time of silent worship, during which the congregants would sit in silent meditation or prayer, listening to the voice of God speaking to them. Often a person would feel "impressed" to share a word with the congregation. This might be what the Lord was saying to him or her personally, or a lesson that person had learned and wanted to share, or it might be a word of admonition to the congregation as a whole. Sometimes a person would just lead out in prayer or quote or read a passage of Scripture. Whatever the situation, there was a sense of the presence of God working in individual lives that impacted the corporate body.

Simply watching and listening to these men and women through the years fostered a discernment of the reality of a living, growing, ongoing personal relationship with Jesus Christ. I learned from them that God does speak to us if we discipline ourselves to listen, expecting to hear from him, and are open to hearing what he has to say through the Scriptures, hymns, or the words of others. I learned that God hears and answers our prayers—not always in the ways we may expect, but in ways that are best for us in the long run.

I also learned about community and fellowship within the body of Christ as I watched and listened to others share their worries, fears, cares, and concerns with one another. I watched them pray for, care for, minister to, and confront one another in love in the midst of life's circumstances. I saw wisdom and experience shared in a loving way with those who did not have either.

One man, Thomas Rule, was a very elderly man from England. He sat in the back pew of our church with his well-worn Bible in his hands, every week wearing the same rumpled blue suit and scrawny tie. As children we laughed at his old-fashioned ways, language, and clothes. Week after week he would stand and share with the congregation what the Lord had spoken to him that morning, usually through the "Sams" (Psalms). He was a rather mysterious old man, and we didn't know much about him, but we never doubted that God was real and had spoken to him. He was very independent and relied on the Lord to meet his needs. He never complained about taking the bus to church, rain or shine, and he never missed a service. His example mentored me.

Louis Hanson was another old saint in our congregation. With his head of white hair and big white beard, he appeared almost like God himself. The gentleness in his eyes, the peace with which he faced the challenges of illness and aging, affirmed what he often stated: "God is faithful, no matter what our outward circumstances may be."

The older women, whose prayers brought the presence of the Holy Spirit into the service, taught me that God is present and our conversations with him are as real and personal as those with our best friends.

Iola, one such woman, had a non-Christian husband and a daughter who was prone to wander far from the Lord. Sunday after Sunday she lifted her voice in prayer, pleading with God

for the salvation of her family. From her I learned perseverance in prayer. Never give up! She didn't, and later in life her
daughter did turn her life over to the Lord. I listened and
watched and learned to pray, not through formal lessons but
by observing the reality of these women's conversations with
God.

I now realize that I was learning from the older people in
my church even when I was a very young child. I can't recall
many particular words that these men and women may have
spoken that directly influenced me. It was more of a sense of
understanding that they knew God and had a personal relationship with him. This helped me see and understand very
early in life that God was real, personal, and interested in all
aspects of my life. I am not sure I would have known it as early
or been able to trust that fact if it had come to me only in
words and not in living example.

I am not alone in this experience. Recently I heard from a
friend in Michigan who happens to be a director of women's
ministries in her church. She, too, has never been formally
mentored. She wrote:

I have never been "officially" mentored by another; yet
have been mentored tens of times through relationships
that run deep.

Annie [a mutual friend] is one of my most meaning-
ful mentors. She has taught me much through the years,
actually before we ever personally met. I can remember
the evening service at Christ Memorial when I first greeted her. She was like a legend. I had heard her speak,
heard much about her from others, and always wanted to

meet her. There she was—standing before me, smiling beautifully, so encouraging and hospitable. She became my mentor as I took over our women's ministry. Over and over her willingness to share from her many experiences gave me the courage to tackle a job that seemed overwhelming at times. She reminds me of the Proverb (11:25, NIV) "[She] who refreshes others will [herself] be refreshed."

Perhaps you, too, can think of one or more people who have mentored you, in an informal sense, over the years. Yet if mentoring is to come outside of a formal arrangement, what is our role in making this happen?

What's My Part?

Growth comes as a personal responsibility. Perhaps you have been looking for a mentor, believing that he or she will have all the answers to your questions and will show you, step-by-step, what you need to do in life. A real mentor, however, is more of a guide, an encourager, one who will challenge you to discover the answers to your questions through a process of seeking and learning yourself. A mentor does not specifically have to be a person with whom you interact verbally. He or she may be a person who has written a book or article that God uses to teach you some new lesson. Your mentor may be a speaker with whom you have no personal interaction. Mentoring happens in the course of everyday activities and chance encounters.

The purpose of this book is to help you discover the resources and recognize the mentors that surround you, wherever you are. It is designed to help you understand that the absence of a particular person as your lifelong personal mentor does not hinder your growth. You can learn from others without a formal mentoring relationship. Furthermore, this book is designed to help you find those persons who can mentor you in short-term relationships for particular needs. It also aims to make you aware of the many "divine interventional" mentoring opportunities that have and will come your way during your life.

Most of all, I want to encourage you, wherever you are. What is key in each situation is maintaining a teachable spirit and developing "mentoring eyes." That means looking for and recognizing divine appointments and growth opportunities as they cross your path, continually seeking out opportunities to learn in everyday situations, whether alone or in a group. It means developing an awareness of the riches of wisdom that are to be found in the simple dailiness of encounters within our work environment, families, communities, and churches. It means living with the expectation that God speaks ... through the still, small voice of the Holy Spirit, in many different ways, through many different people, past, present, personal, and even through the media of books, tapes, speakers, movies, radio, and television.

We need to realize that there is not just one way to gain the empowerment of personal growth and effectiveness; there are many. Many teaching voices will surround us throughout our lives, and if our eyes, ears, hearts, and minds are open we will discover the various ways God will lead us on to becoming all he created us to be. As Mary Ann R. Hershey has said, "the key to a vital life is an eagerness to learn and a willingness to change."[2]

So how can we become aware of the "teaching voices" that surround us? Who will be our guide on the path to change and growth? The next chapter will help you learn to develop "mentoring eyes," so that you can begin to recognize the many mentors already surrounding you.

As a first step, however, here is a simple tool to help you determine who has already made a difference in your life.

1. Name the five wealthiest people in the world.
2. Name the last five Heisman trophy winners.
3. Name the last five winners of the Miss America contest.
4. Name ten people who have won the Nobel Peace Prize.
5. Name the last six Academy Award winners in the best actress or actor category.
6. Name the last ten years' World Series winners.

How did you do? The point is, none of us remember the headliners of yesterday, even though they are the best in their fields. Here's another quiz; see how you do on this one.

1. List a few teachers who aided your journey through school.
2. Name three friends who have helped you through a difficult time.
3. Name five people who have taught you something worthwhile.
4. Think of a few people who have made you feel special and appreciated.

5. Think of five people with whom you enjoy spending time.
6. Name several heroes whose stories have inspired you.

Was this easier? The people who make a difference in your life are not usually the ones with the best credentials, the most money, or the biggest awards. They are the ones who care, the ones whose lives you have watched, the ones from whom you have learned. These are your mentors.

Personal Evaluation

1. Who, in your past, has been a mentor by example?
2. What resources are available to you right now?

CHAPTER THREE

Look Around

The last to board the plane from Seattle to Dallas were a woman and three children. *Oh, please don't sit next to me,* Dan Begley thought, *I've got so much work to do.*

A moment later, however, an eleven-year-old girl and her nine-year-old brother were climbing over me while the woman and a four-year-old boy sat behind. Almost immediately the older children started bickering, while the child behind intermittently kicked my seat. Every few minutes the older boy would ask his sister, "Where are we now?" "Shut up!" she'd snap, and a new round of squirming and whining would ensue.

Kids have no concept of important work, I thought, quietly resenting my predicament. Then in my mind a voice as clear as a song simply said, *"Love them."*

These kids are brats, and I've got important work to do, I countered to myself. My inner voice simply replied, *Love them as if they were your children.*

Having heard the "Where-are-we-now?" question repeatedly, I turned to the in-flight magazine map, in spite of my important work.

I explained our flight path, dividing it into quarter-hour

flight increments, and estimated when we would land in Dallas.

Soon they were telling me about their trip to Seattle to see their father, who was in the hospital. As we talked they asked about flying, navigation, science, and grown-ups' views about life. The time passed quickly and my "important" work was left undone.

As we were preparing to land, I asked how their father was doing now. They grew quiet and the boy simply said, "He died."

"Oh, I'm so sorry."

"Yeah, me too. But it's my little brother I'm most worried about. He's taking it real hard."

I suddenly realized what we'd really been talking about was the most important work we'd ever face: living, loving, and growing in spite of heartbreak. When we said good-bye in Dallas the boy shook my hand and thanked me for being his "airline teacher." And I thanked him for being mine.[1]

The last thing Dan Begley was looking for as he boarded that plane was the chance to become a mentor, and to be mentored in return. Yet God knew that was exactly what he, and those children, needed at that very moment. Because Dan was willing to open his mind to what God was saying, this important moment was not lost.

Indeed, if we are willing to listen, God is continually bringing learning opportunities into our lives. "In him lie hidden all the mighty, untapped treasures of wisdom and knowledge," Paul says in Colossians 2:3 (LB). Yet hidden treasures imply a searching on our part to discover them. Peter shows us one way that we can find those treasures: "As you know him better, he will give you, through his great power, *everything you need* for living a truly good life: he even shares his own glory and his own goodness with us! And by that same mighty power, he has given us all the other rich and wonderful blessings he promised" (2 Pt 1:3-4, LB; italics mine).

The phrase *everything you need* is included in almost every translation of 2 Peter 1:3. God, himself, the ultimate mentor, wants to make you able to reflect his very character. So he doesn't leave you frustrated or without the guidance and direction you need. He supplies it. Sometimes it is through a person and a mentoring relationship; sometimes it is in unexpected ways and places. The challenge for us is to learn how to put the promises and gifts God has given us into practice in our lives and to recognize the learning opportunities God places in our paths. This is where we need to begin to develop "mentoring eyes," to begin to look for and see the provisions of God that surround us.

Mentoring Eyes

How do we develop mentoring eyes? We discipline ourselves to look for lessons in everyday situations. Jesus and his disciples taught lessons by example, stories, principles, and parables. Those lessons often seemed hidden to casual hearers. Even the disciples would sometimes miss the point he was making.

When Jesus was teaching the multitudes the principle of

sowing seeds in good soil, no one seemed to quite understand the point he was making. Not even his disciples understood. So they asked him not only what he meant but why he spoke so often in parables. He replied, "The knowledge of the secrets of the kingdom of heaven has been given to you, but not to them. Though seeing, they do not see, though hearing, they do not hear or understand. In them is fulfilled the prophecy of Isaiah: 'You will be ever hearing but never understanding; you will be ever seeing but never perceiving. For this people's heart has become calloused; they hardly hear with their ears, and they have closed their eyes'" (Mt 13:11, 13-15, NIV).

Our world is much like that of the first century. We have so much worldly wisdom that often we believe we know it all. Many believe, as did Karl Marx, that "religion is the opiate of the people." Education, common sense, and sophistication may make us think we know it all. Arrogance may keep us from seeing and hearing the simple message of God's love and forgiveness. The discipline and commitment needed to become a disciple of Jesus Christ don't seem to hold much appeal to modern-day society. This can hinder our discovery of the "hidden treasures" of Christ's teachings.

Yet all around us there are those who have discovered the secrets of Jesus' power and his promises that surround us. They have put into practice the very lessons we need to learn. These are the ones who are actively looking. They can be examples and teachers to us.

We may believe that we have eyes that see, yet we live life at such a fast pace that many times we are not even aware of what is going on around us. Often we miss the lessons available to us on a day-to-day basis. We miss the teachable moments that surround us because we are not looking for them. This is not because our hearts are hard, but rather because we are consumed in the crises of the moment. We all get caught up in the daily details of life, and it can hinder our seeing the bigger plan God has for us. Our immediate problems overwhelm us and seem to obliterate God's promises. God, on the other hand, sees the bigger picture and wants us to focus in on what he is accomplishing in our lives. God's lessons are surrounding us daily, if only we are willing to set aside our busyness and open our "eyes to see and ears to hear."

Look Around

Florence Littauer, in her Christian Leaders, Authors, Speakers Seminars (CLASS), emphasizes the importance of being what she calls "Alert to Life." She means that we need to be aware of what is going on in the world around us, keeping up to date with the news headlines, the books, and other media that are influencing our culture, as well as noticing the things that surround us that we so often take for granted.

As seekers and learners I believe we need to be "alert to life" by becoming aware of the lessons that present themselves every day. These little daily lessons form our character. Our daughter, Susan, related one such lesson to us.

Flying to New Zealand with two- and five-year-old toddlers was no fun! Susan had brought every toy and book she felt would keep the children entertained on the fifteen-hour flight. Yet the children had long since become bored. Holding, walking, singing—nothing seemed to quiet them down or get them to sleep. Finally, about an hour before landing, the children, exhausted, fell asleep, as did Sue.

As they began their descent into Auckland, the flight attendant began making the preliminary landing announcements. After going through all the immigration details, she gave her final bit of advice.

"As you leave your seats, be sure that you look around and *uplift all your personal belongings.*"

Susan looked over at her two adorable little children, sleeping soundly like little angels. Her mind went back to her impatience with them during the flight. She remembered the sternness in her voice and the frustration she had shown when they wouldn't behave as adults. The flight attendant's words struck home, as Susan realized that Elizabeth and Andrew were her most precious "personal belongings." God taught her a lesson that morning through the words, "uplift all your personal belongings."

For the next two weeks as they visited relatives and traveled, seeing friends, every time Susan was tempted to expect Elizabeth and Andrew to act like adults, instead of letting her impatience win out, she did her best to *"uplift"* her precious children.

Susan was alert to life and to the lessons God was teaching through the simple instructions meant to remind people not to leave anything on the airplane.

Can words spoken to mean one thing have a very different meaning and impact for some? I think Susan would say "yes," if we are open to learning lessons and "alert to life." God spoke to Susan through the everyday instructions of a flight attendant.

As we develop "mentoring eyes," the habit of intentionally looking for lessons in everyday life, we will find that many "teachable moments" surround us.

My friend Delores told of an occasion when an unexpected mentor surprised her husband.

She is known as a sweet, godly lady, somewhat lacking in verbal skills, namely the ability to get to the point. When in a Bible study group with her I did discover that when she is given the opportunity to complete her thought, it is usually PROFOUND! However, since this exercise requires more patience than most people possess, she is rarely completely heard, often interrupted and passed over in group conversation.

Last Monday she called to talk with my husband, who always gets a bit antsy when conversing with her, but is much too polite to not hear her out. At the end of the call, he appeared stunned. Knowing he was to fill in for the teacher of our Sunday school class the following Sunday, she was calling "to encourage him." Understand: he teaches graduate students for a living and has a string of degrees, though he actually didn't have a clue where to go with the general topic he'd been given. He told me he just let her talk, but then started jotting down notes after her introductory remarks, and by the time she signed off, he had his outline for Sunday. It was delivered yesterday and was so well received that he was requested to do a sequel next Sunday. He plans to publicly give her credit for the outline at the close. Reaction of the class should be interesting!

How often have you been surprised by an unexpected "nugget of truth" from an unlikely source? Take a few moments and try to recall some lesson that you may have learned from an unexpected source. Then begin to intentionally start looking for lessons in the daily encounters of life.

Personal Evaluation

1. In what areas of your life do you need help or advice?
2. Can you think of someone who might be able to guide you in each of these areas?

CHAPTER FOUR

Look for Role Models

The object of our search must be not only the unexpected "mentoring moments" in life, but also the men and women who are role models in the skills and traits we would like to learn. Jesus himself is an example of this, for it was his traits and skills that first attracted the disciples to become his followers.

Indeed, it was while going about their daily activities that the disciples learned the most from Jesus. He taught by his example as they walked from place to place, pondering on everyday things and occurrences. This was very different than the traditional method of learning. Learning in that day followed a very formal ritual. The rabbi or teacher would gather a few students around him and pour information into them, testing them by questions to see how well they had learned. This opportunity was offered to only the privileged few. Jesus didn't limit his teaching to just the disciples, however; he welcomed the masses, including the outcasts, even the women, who were never considered worthy to be "learners" in first-century society. He taught wherever he was, meeting each situation as it arose, and gleaning lessons to be passed on to those around him.

Many of us may have had the advantages of higher learning

and traditional teaching methods. Yet most would agree that the most practical lessons learned have come through observing and interacting with others. Look around and find those who seem to be skilled and knowledgeable in the areas in which you wish to learn and grow. Find ways to spend time with these people, observing and interacting, if possible.

As a young woman I wanted to share Jesus Christ with friends and neighbors. I not only wanted to share the message of salvation, but I had a real desire to encourage others in their spiritual growth. I felt very inadequate and untrained. I had no Bible college or seminary training. Yet, I was an eager learner. I took advantage of every Bible class and seminar our church offered. I looked for and attended seminars, retreats, revivals, and classes that were offered in our area. I gleaned bits and pieces from all of them. Probably, though, I learned the most from our pastor's wife, who led our women's Bible study and couples' Sunday school class. I learned by observing how much time and effort she put into studying and preparing for each lesson. I saw how reverently she treated the Scriptures, careful always to be sure that she was not taking verses out of context. I watched her draw practical lessons with concrete instructions that helped us put into practice the points she made. Now, thirty-five years later, having graduated from seminary and taught Bible studies myself for over twenty years, I realize the basic principles of my teaching were learned, not in seminary, but from Martha Davidson. She was my mentor, though we never called it that, nor did we ever have formal discussions on the topic of teaching.

Today, I am still looking around for mentors from whom I can learn the skills I need. Marita Littauer, who is considerably younger than I, is very gifted in areas of creative marketing. She is also computer savvy! I want to present materials at my seminars and retreats that are attractive and helpful and look professional. I am learning from her. Marita is my mentor in areas in which she has stronger natural gifts, plus more experience and training. Yet she is younger than I. Mentors do not have to be older. They just need to be people who know something we don't.

Nor are mentors only for our professional or spiritual growth. Mothers of Preschoolers (MOPS) is an organization that is designed to help young mothers find companionship and assistance in the raising of young children. Each MOPS group has an older woman as an advisor. She is called a "Mentor Mom." These mentor moms meet with the young women every week, not in a teaching capacity, but rather as someone to whom the women can turn with questions on most any subject. They are not highly trained moms, except by virtue of their experience, from which they are willing to share guidance, love, and support to young moms with questions and needs.

Asking for Help

In past generations, when we did not have the "advantage" of television and so many self-help books and tapes, it was common for men and women to go to their friends and family for advice and help in specific situations. Today we have become so transient, living apart from extended family, in neighborhoods that don't provide the closeness they once did, that we don't have those natural, comfortable relationships which provide the mentoring and modeling we need. We have to be proactive, seeking the persons who may be able to give us a new perspective on our situation.

We must be aware, however, as we seek those who may provide us with some of the answers we need, that many who might be considered mentors by virtue of their age and experience do not consider themselves qualified. They may initially be reluctant to give advice. It is important when you approach someone for help that you make it very clear that you are asking only for that person's advice. Don't approach a potential mentor with the expectation that he or she will have all the answers to your needs. Let that person know why you have chosen to come to him or her. It might be your observation of and respect for the way he or she has parented, or for his or her obvious commitment to marriage, or ability to ... whatever it is for which you are seeking help.

Though Tara and Mike had known their friends Rita and Bob for several years, they had become good friends only when both husbands were transferred to California and they began doing things socially together. Out of that grew a friendship. Because Rita had older sons, Tara found herself discussing her teenagers with Rita. Rita would often share what she had done when her boys were teenagers, including her mistakes. In time they joined a Bible study, and even began praying together. Tara began to respect Rita's advice as she observed their common values and commitment. While neither Rita nor Bob would probably use the term "mentors" to explain their relationship with Tara and Mike, in specific areas it has become that.

Looking for mentors for specific needs on a short-term basis is a good beginning point to discover your own responsiveness to this type of relationship as well as discover the right person or persons for future mentoring. Often time constraints may hinder a potential mentor's willingness to get involved. Make it clear that you are not particularly looking for a long-term mentoring relationship. It may grow into that as you connect and discover this person has experience and good advice not only in the initial area for which you consulted him or her, but also on life itself. Going in with long-term expectations, however, may overwhelm the potential mentor. You may also find that you and your potential mentor just don't "click." Seeking a mentor for a specific situation will give you the opportunity to discover if this person is someone with whom you would like to foster a longer term or more formal mentoring relationship.

I myself have been a part of such a short-term arrangement which has evolved into a more formal relationship. It began at an extremely busy period in my life. I was scheduled for surgery the following week, and three weeks later we would be moving from our home into a rental. I was teaching at a seminar, and one attendee seemed to need more of my time and attention than I expected. She was new in our area and lonely, but I just didn't have time for any more relationships! However, she offered to help in any way she could during the move, and when my recuperation turned out to be much harder and longer than I anticipated, I took her up on her offer. Her help in unpacking and arranging my books, plus the delicious meal she prepared, opened the door for an ongoing relationship.

That was five years ago. Pam and I meet occasionally for lunch, sharing what is going on in our lives. We communicate by e-mail, and I read and give suggestions as she endeavors to become a published author. I listen to her taped messages, or look over outlines for retreats. I have become one of Pam's mentors. If she had asked directly for mentoring at that busy point in my life five years ago, I would have simply said "no." Yet her willingness to help me, no strings attached, led to a relationship that has evolved into mentoring. Like most mentors, I am also learning from Pam.

Susan Foster discovered a mentor when, being intrigued by a Bible study topic advertised in her local area, she decided to attend. The teacher became that mentor. "She took a real interest in me and provided me with spiritual insights. She gave me wise and godly counsel. She affirmed and encouraged me. I was devastated when she moved away. Yet that was not the end of our mentoring relationship. Through her input I had 'an encounter with Christ.' I relinquished myself, body and soul, to Christ's lordship and became his disciple. Ever since, he has been working in my life. I know now that God orchestrated our meeting to bring me to him."

Susan wasn't looking for a mentor; she didn't even know she needed one. Yet God knew ... and he brought Susan just the person she needed to lead Susan to him.

Look around at your current relationships. Is there someone with whom you have contact who is skilled in areas in which you wish to grow? Are there skills you have that that person may need? Perhaps, like Pam, you can do something for that person that will free up enough of his or her time to allow him or her to help you in specific areas. Is there someone among your acquaintances who may have already experienced a situation similar to yours? See if you can find that person, and then go to him or her for advice. Make it clear to a potential mentor specifically what type of help you need and why you believe he or she can meet that need. This will help that person understand that "mentoring" you does not have to be a lifetime commitment.

Always keep in mind the character and reputation of the person from whom you ask advice. Be sure it is someone whose values are similar to yours. We know the world is full of advice-givers on all subjects, but not all of the advice given lines up with truth, our values, or morality. Ask God to bring to mind the right person to ask for help.

God has promised us everything we need, and we can find the fulfillment of his promises all around us. We only need to take the time and make the effort to develop mentoring eyes. Look around you; you will be amazed at the blessings you find.

Personal Evaluation

1. Who has been a role model for you in the past? Who is a role model for you now?
2. Identify the people in your life who have shown you how to do something very specific, even if they couldn't have served as a mentor in a broad sense.

CHAPTER FIVE

Look Back

The phone rang. "Would you please meet and pray with me?" I was surprised to hear those words coming from Ruth. Ruth was a few years older than I, the mother of six little girls. Her house was always spotless. She made most of her children's clothes as well as her own. Her cooking was unsurpassed. She and her husband were the presidents of our young married couples Sunday school class. Her children were very well behaved. She was the epitome of all I aspired to be as a wife, mother, and Christian woman. I thought Ruth was aptly named after the biblical character, for she seemed to be as unselfish and as hard a worker as Ruth of the Scriptures. Why would she call and ask me to pray *with her?* Puzzled, but very flattered to be asked, I agreed to meet with her to pray.

That was the beginning of a routine that has changed my life. I suppose that simple request has made me who I am today. I was very interested in prayer, and had watched and listened to the prayers of the men and women of my home church, but I didn't really know if I knew how to pray. Having someone whom I so admired come to me and ask me to pray with her was what God used to open me up to a whole new understanding of prayer. Ruth and I began to meet weekly to share our family concerns and to pray with and for each other.

With my three toddlers and her six, ranging in age from six to twelve, it was a real struggle to find the time to get together and have enough peace and quiet to pray. However, we made it a priority. Week in and week out, we prayed, over little problems and big ones. As we began to see answers, our faith grew. We read books on prayer; we listened and watched others pray. We were hungry to know more about prayer. From that moment over forty years ago, having a personal prayer partner has been a must for my spiritual growth.

As my family has made each of its moves across this country, I have prayed for God to send me a new prayer partner. Each time he has brought exactly the right person into my life. My prayer partners are an extremely important part of my spiritual life. We challenge and confront one another. We hold each other accountable. We laugh and cry, celebrate and commiserate, but most of all we pray—for each other, our spouses, our children, their mates, our grandchildren, our parents, our family members, and our friends. I am still close to each of my former prayer partners, though we live far apart. Looking back, I see that a simple telephone call and request sent me into a lifetime of accountability and prayer. Isn't it amazing how such a simple thing can change a life?

Even more importantly, the call that began a pattern of prayer in my life was like a pebble thrown into the pond. Our daughters watched as I met weekly with my prayer partner. They knew that Mommy wasn't to be disturbed when she was praying. My youngest daughter, Kristi, told me recently that just watching my prayer partner and me take the time to pray has made a big difference in her life.

Mom, you really modeled Scripture for me. I saw the power of "where two or three are gathered in my name" (Mt 18:20, RSV). I learned the importance of corporate prayer. I also noticed that you always made time for your prayer. To me, it seemed like a long time as I watched the two of you praying. I could tell that your prayer time was as much a priority as your time for shopping, cleaning, sewing, and the other "must-do" things of life. Sometimes I listened and heard your specific prayers for me. I was embarrassed occasionally as I realized what you had shared ... but I was also glad that both of you cared and were praying for me. Because of that I have always felt closer to your prayer partners than other friends.

Furthermore, I believe that watching you pray with another has made it so much easier for Bill and me to pray together. We started doing that when we were dating, and because I was used to seeing two people pray regularly it made it easier for me. The impact of that doesn't stop with my generation. I was hosting a Moms In Touch group at my home recently, when the phone rang. Briana, our five-year-old, answered the phone.

"Mommy is praying right now and can't be disturbed. May I take a message?"

I smiled inwardly as my thoughts went back to the days when I was Briana's age and knew that Mommy was praying and couldn't be interrupted.

I didn't realize during those years that my choice to make prayer time a priority was anything more than a nuisance to my girls. I just knew that I desperately needed that time. I would never have initiated such a relationship when I was so young and insecure. But I know beyond a shadow of a doubt that I would not be who I am today if it had not been for the many "mentoring moments" that have come through those three prayer partners. One request, by someone who I admired, has no doubt been used by God to change, not only my life, but generations of all of our families. Yet I see now that I was mentoring by my example, and the effects of that example continue to spread through the generations of my family.

Mentoring isn't just something that happens outside of family relationships. So often we relegate it to business, social, or ministry situations. In so doing we may miss some of the best lessons life has for us. Our families have wisdom and experience that can greatly benefit us if we are open to hearing and receiving their advice. The world would have missed a great deal of wisdom had not a young boy been willing to listen and follow his father's advice, as told in the following true story.

It was an eighth-grade school graduation, and in that small farming community, no one gave much in the way of graduation gifts. A crumpled two-dollar bill and a card were John's only gifts. John's father wasn't a man for fancy speeches or gifts. But that simple gift and his example have echoed down through the generations, impacting thousands of lives.

"As long as you have this you will never be broke," John's father said as he handed John the two-dollar bill. Then he pulled out a card on which he had written "Guidelines for life." No lecture. These were just the guidelines by which he had lived. He wanted his son to know that the most valuable thing he could ever acquire was virtue.

"Son, try to live up to these things."

On one side of the card was a poem by Henry Van Dyke. It was a short rhyme that reminded John to think clearly, love sincerely, act purely, and trust God securely. Then on the flip side was his father's personal creed. The top of the card read: "Seven things to do." John knew the seven things—he had seen them in action every single day of his life. But now he had them in writing. Something about seeing it on the card made a lasting impression on the boy. The list read:

Be true to yourself.
Help others.
Make each day your masterpiece.
Drink deeply from good books, especially the Bible.
Make friendship a fine art.
Build a shelter against a rainy day.
Pray for guidance, count and give thanks for your
    blessings every day.

For over seventy years John Wooden has carried that card and the two-dollar bill his father gave him. And he has done his best to live by his father's seven rules.

As coach of the UCLA basketball team for twenty-seven years, John has passed down his virtues and values to hundreds of men. NBA Hall-of-Famer and former UCLA basketball player Bill Walton said, "I was touched by

Coach Wooden's greatness—he set a standard I have been trying to live up to ever since. He is as positive as you get. He taught values and characteristics that could make us not only good players but good people. I'm telling my four teenage sons what he used to tell his players. I'm even writing his maxims on their lunch bags."[1]

I recently saw Coach Wooden on public television, sharing and expanding on the seven things his father taught him. I was impressed by the presence of the man. His words were simple but full of wisdom. His face mirrored a man at peace with God and himself. He is a man who has gained the respect of the nation. He is a man who has been an example and mentor to many players, coaches, sportswriters, and broadcasters. Beyond that, to all who have observed, he has shown by his example his faith in God. As his father mentored him, by his silent example, Coach Wooden has mentored all whose lives he has touched.

As we look back to our pasts, for many of us our earliest mentoring experiences were found within our own families. Though we, and they, may not have realized it at the time, the examples set by the members of our families—and likewise those we set today for our youngest family members—echo down through the generations.

Personal Evaluation

1. Who in your past has seen value in you?
2. How has this person's belief in you made a difference in your life?

CHAPTER SIX

Look for Turning Points

Mentoring moments may not be prolonged, but when someone whom you respect says just the right words or gives you
attention when you need it the most, the effect can last a lifetime. These are life's turning points.

One man shared with me how, when he was a young, insecure kid from a troubled family, a neighborhood youth pastor
took an interest in him. Every Monday afternoon the pastor
would pick him up at school and take him to McDonald's. He
doesn't remember much of what they talked about, and he
even lost track of the man after high school. Yet looking back
he realized that the fact that the pastor cared enough to spend
time and money on him, a skinny kid who seemed to have no
future, marked the beginning of his believing that he could
amount to something. The more he thought about the impact
that man had made on him, the more he felt led to find that
pastor and thank him. He finally tracked him down and went
to visit him. The pastor had recently been forced into retire-
ment, and as he reflected back on his over fifty years in ministry, he felt as if he had been a failure. He had never built a
mega-church, written a book, or done any of the things by
which we measure success. He had just been a faithful pastor,
performing his duties, caring for the people, and occasionally

taking a junior high kid out for snacks.

Yet the man who came back to thank this pastor has gone on to success in ministry and education. He firmly believes that if it hadn't been for the faithful caring of that pastor those many years ago, he would have followed the failing footsteps of those in his family who never completed their education or stayed with any one job, and most often ended up in prison.

In this case it wasn't so much the words that were said as the fact that someone paid attention to a kid whom no one else thought was worth much or had much of a chance in life. Yet the effect was life-changing.

Trudy

My friend Trudy is another example of mentoring at life's turning points. Trudy was the fourth child born to a Dutch family. She had two older sisters, and her birth followed closely behind that of the long-awaited son of the family. Trudy was not given much encouragement and tended to be a sickly child. However, music was very important to the family, and thinking it might help Trudy, they asked the pastor's daughter to give Trudy piano lessons.

One day Trudy's pastor asked, "Trudy, will you please play the piano when the children are dismissed from the worship service to Sunday school?" Trudy was only eleven years old.

"But I don't know any hymns; all I know are my simple beginning songs."

"I will help you find a simple hymn with no flats or sharps. You can do it," were her teacher, Miss Mary June's, encouraging words. Kerplunk, kerplunk, a few Sundays later, Trudy pounded out the simple tune, "I Gave My Life for Thee."

Each Sunday Trudy's playing improved, as did her self-confidence. When Trudy was fifteen years old she played a Rachmaninoff concerto to dedicate the new Steinway piano for the school where her piano teacher taught.

Trudy's involvement in church also began at that early age. The encouragement her piano teacher gave her carried over into making missions presentations for the Sunday school. She has gone on to serve in many areas, including being the director of women's ministries at the Crystal Cathedral for over twenty years.

"Betty," she told me, "that pastor and his daughter's attention and trust in me opened the door to my being in ministry today. They gave me the gift of believing in me. That helped me learn to believe in myself."

Peter

Have you ever had any one whose persistent and consistent belief in your gifts, talents, skills, or character finally gave you the courage to begin believing in yourself? I have!

I am so grateful to the many different people I can recall from my past who saw something in me that I did not see in myself. We are often harder on ourselves than others are on us. Watching others, who by their words and actions kept reinforcing my abilities and character, freed me to reassess my view of myself and set me on the path to becoming the woman they seemed to see in me.

The apostle Peter was someone whom I believe evolved into a better man because Jesus believed so strongly in what he saw hidden in the depths of Peter's character. We know Peter as an impulsive person: "Open mouth, insert foot." How often I have empathized with him. Jesus' first words to Peter were, "Come, follow me" (Mk 1:17, NIV). His last words to him were, "*You* follow me" (Jn 21:22, NKJV). In between the first and last words of the Lord to Peter were many ups and downs in their relationship. From the moment Jesus entered Peter's life, this plain fisherman became a new person with new goals and priorities. Yet he was not perfect, and many times along the way he stumbled. Peter was the only disciple who had faith enough to step out of the boat and walk on the water toward Jesus, but Peter also became afraid and took his eyes off Jesus. He then began to sink beneath the waves. Jesus reached out and rescued Peter.

A little later Jesus asked his disciples, "Who do you think I am?" Peter answered, "The Christ, the Messiah, the Son of the living God" (Mt 16:15-16, LB). Peter took a strong stand that day, and Jesus called him a "rock." Yet only a few days later, Peter, seeking to protect Jesus from the suffering he prophesied, took him aside to remonstrate with him. "Jesus turned on Peter and said, 'Get away from me, you Satan! You are a dangerous trap to me. You are thinking merely from a human point of view, and not from God's'" (Mt 16:23, LB).

Again, at the Transfiguration, Peter blurted out, wanting to act, to do something. Jesus wanted his worship, not his actions. Oh, how I relate. It is so much easier for me to find something to do for the Lord then it is to sit and worship him.

Yet Jesus still loved and saw value in Peter. Throughout Jesus' ministry Peter was there, alternating between wise and foolish actions. Right up to the time of Jesus' arrest Peter assured the Lord he would stick by him and not fail him. Yet within a few hours Peter denied three times that he knew

Jesus. Still, one of the first things Jesus did after his resurrection was to find Peter and forgive him. Peter denied Jesus three times, and three times Jesus asked Peter if he loved him. Jesus removed the cloud of guilt Peter felt (see Jn 21:15-22, NIV). Peter went on to become a great evangelist, still not perfect, but effective in his ministry.

Kristi and Gail

I, myself, have seen the effect a little encouragement can have on a person caught at one of life's turning points. When we were transferred to California from Arizona, our two oldest daughters were away in college. Kristi, our youngest, was just entering high school. She found the California lifestyle to be very different. She also had trouble finding her place in a youth group. She missed her friends and home church. I was very concerned for her, as I saw her becoming more and more discouraged and depressed.

Gail Wenos, a Christian ventriloquist and speaker, was a member of our local church. She had given several performances at functions that I had attended. Kristi had been interested in ventriloquism since she had been a little girl, and had her own ventriloquist's dummy. I asked Gail if she would be willing to give Kristi some performance tips. Gail generously agreed to do so. She called Kristi and asked her to come with her to a Mother/Daughter event where Gail would be performing. Kristi was both very excited and intimidated. Here is what Kristi told me recently.

We went out to lunch together before the event. I was so nervous being with someone famous that I kept spilling things. But Gail really put me at ease. She was so open, humble, kind, and helpful. She shared with me her story. She, too, had struggled with low self-esteem. Ezra, her dummy, has become her alter ego. He allows her to say and do things she would never have the courage to do herself. She helped me understand that I could overcome my fears if I was willing to put in the time and effort. She encouraged my performances. When I told her I had trouble writing scripts and coming up with clever and funny things to say, she simply said, "copy mine." Gail became a role model and mentor to me.

Ann

Sometimes mentoring moments come about to help us face things from which we have been hiding. Ann told me her story:

About twenty-seven years ago, nine years after my pastor husband left our family, I still lived with my fantasy of his return.... A dear friend, who had been watching me hanging on, hoping for his return, said to me: "I have a story to tell you," and he continued: "There was a little girl named Ann, and she had a tragedy in her life. She built a memorial to that tragedy, and now she's walking round and round and round that tragedy. Ann, when are you going to bury the corpse?" That encounter had a profound impact on me, and I began to pray—"OK, Lord, I'm ready for whatever or whoever you have ready for me"—and six months later I met Lee!

Lee and Ann have been married for twenty-five years now. Yet Ann realizes that she needed to hear those fairly harsh words to let go of the past and let God prepare her for the future.

Miss Bea

At other times mentoring moments come about just because someone takes the time to show they care. Miss Bea, a young woman in her early twenties, was the superintendent of the Bible Sunday school in a small neighborhood church in Los Angeles. She was also the Bible school teacher for preteenage girls.

The summer Cate was twelve, during her birthday week, she came down with the German measles, which lasted two weeks. She had to stay inside in a darkened room to protect her eyes.

After a few days, Miss Bea came to visit, and Cate was delighted.

She brought me the lessons I would miss, and we went over them. She also prayed for me. The Sunday I returned to Bible school she asked me to be her helper: "Will you please pass out the lessons?" I was thrilled and felt very needed.

When Miss Bea was planning her wedding, she asked eight of us girls to practice as her bridesmaids. We were delighted and felt very important. I stayed in her Bible classes until I was eighteen, when I was asked to be the leader of the Bible school. I became a leader because of my mentor, Miss Bea.

Looking back to the early influences and the turning points in our lives, even the negative ones, can reveal how God has been divinely intervening in our lives, bringing just the right message at just the right time. Sometimes a family member has been the one to carry that message; other times it may have been a friend, a pastor, a teacher, or even a stranger with a kind word. Reflecting on these important points in our lives can help us focus on where we have been, where we are now, and where we want to go. The next chapters will illustrate how looking up expectantly to God can bring clarity to our future.

Personal Evaluation

1. Think about and describe a "turning point" in your life.
2. What difference has this made?

CHAPTER SEVEN

Look Into Books

Up to this point we have concentrated on looking for mentors with whom we have had direct interaction. However, some of my most powerful mentors have been people whom I have never met. I think of these people as part of "the great cloud of witnesses" that the book of Hebrews tells us "surrounds us" (Heb 12:1, NIV) and I believe that God, through the Holy Spirit, quickens to my heart the lessons I need to hear that come from their experience. We can listen to the voices of people with whom we never have any personal interaction. They speak to us in books, on the public platform, on the radio, or in God's Word.

Books are wonderful mentors; they are available at any hour of the day or night. We can reread them and glean new insights throughout our lives. No doubt God has spoken to me through books more than through any other source.

I shared in earlier chapters the examples of the men and women who surrounded me, making an impact in my early years. Not only did I learn from watching them, I also learned the blessings that come from reading and studying Christian literature from ages past. As a little girl, my escape was often reading. I loved to frequent our church library and find books that told the exciting stories of missionaries living in exotic foreign places. I learned many lessons from the biographies or stories of past heroes of the faith.

Isobel Kuhn's stories of her work in China captured my imagination. Her personal journey from doubt to faith, told in *By Searching*, helped me come to terms with my own struggles and doubts. I still have copies of four of her books written in the late 1940s and 1950s. I dream of going to China and seeing the area in which she lived and worked. Missions came alive as I read the stories of the Lisu people, their heartaches, struggles, and faith. Her writings mentored me in perseverance and prayer. To this day I am thrilled and challenged by the stories of men and women who obey God's calling on their lives in the midst of life's most trying circumstances.

Book Mentors

As I was writing this book, I took from my bookshelf some books written by my favorite authors from the past. These writings have made an impact on my life. I wanted to reread some of their works, to discover if they still speak to me. Catherine Marshall has always been a favorite "book mentor." Taking a break from writing, I picked up a collection of her writings, *The Best of Catherine Marshall*, and turned to the section, "Dark Night of the Soul." A series of negative events had come into her life, culminating with the terminal illness and death of her namesake granddaughter, Amy Catherine. Catherine was sure that she had heard God tell her that Amy would be healed. She had gathered friends and family from around the nation to pray continuously for Amy, and was claiming, with all her heart and faith, Amy's healing. When Amy died, Catherine was both devastated and humiliated, because she had stated so strongly that God had told her Amy would not die. She was also angry with God and began a slide into deep depression that nothing seemed to break. A year later, Catherine's husband and two of her dearest friends gathered in her home for an intervention to try to break through Catherine's depression.

As I read her account of the questions with which they confronted her, I began to identify some thought patterns that were hindering my own freedom and fullness of God's Spirit. These are the words she wrote with which I identified:

Understanding. That seems to be the key word in my difficulties. I have sought it from the Lord most of my life; in His gentle tenderness He has often provided it. So often, in fact, that I had begun to take it for granted. I assumed I had a right to understanding. What arrogance! What presumption!

Then a new thought hit me like a thunderbolt: Presumption was my sin. Had I really heard Him say what His plan was for her? Or had I wanted the healing so badly I simply imagined that He must, too? Presumption. I had assumed something I had no right to assume. God will always be God. We will never fathom His ways, but I presumed to try. "O Lord, forgive me for my presumption."

Then still another thought struck me. Worse than my presumption, even, is the fact that with Amy Catherine I had really wanted to play God, to be God in her life. I tried to usurp the power of almighty God. "O Lord, can you forgive me for this abomination?"

And He answered me. At long, long last, I heard the

Voice that had been silent for so many months: *I, your God, am in everything. The baby died, but Amy Catherine is with ME. And while she lived, she ministered to everyone who prayed for her. You alone, Catherine, were too stubborn to see it.*[1]

As I read Catherine's confession, the Lord spoke to my heart and helped me see where I, too, had been presumptuous in a matter over which I had been praying for the past year. I wanted to take control of a situation and I certainly did not understand why God had allowed certain things to occur. How faithful God is to break through our stubborn resistance. By his divine intervention, once again God had used Catherine Marshall's writings to mentor me.

Catherine Marshall's books have not only mentored me through the years, but God has also used them to totally change Susan's life. Here is her story.

We don't always choose our mentors. In many instances, such as my own, we may never meet them except through history or books. In my case, God unexpectedly dropped a mentor into my life in a miraculous way when I needed the guidance the most. My life would never be the same. I consider it one of His greatest gifts to me.

In my twenties, I had achieved everything I thought I had wanted in life: a successful career, a sports car, a charming house, beautiful clothes, a handsome, successful husband, and a social life. Having grown up in Christian homes, my husband and I attended church on Sundays, but after a while we found the services rather dull, and eventually we drifted away.

By the time I reached my late twenties, my life had slowly begun to unravel: my marriage, my career, an illness, emotional problems, and by thirty, a strong-willed child who seemed to be running my life. Now I needed God, and I began desperately seeking him, but he was silent.

One dismal afternoon, I was standing in a long line at the laundry on the verge of tears, feeling hopeless. Meg, my two-year-old daughter, wiggled away from me to inspect a stack of books in the corner. Not wanting to lose my place in line, I decided to let her explore.

Suddenly I heard a loud crash and Meg's scream! I rushed over to uncover my toddler from the avalanche of books. Before I could stop her, she grabbed a book and gleefully ripped off the cover. I grabbed the damaged merchandise, wondering what kind of book I had just unwillingly purchased! *Something More*, by Catherine Marshall, I said aloud. *Well, I certainly need something more,* I thought ... *maybe this is no accident.*

Later that evening, I flipped through *Something More*, noting it was a Christian book, and tossed it into the garbage. I wasn't interested in reading a Christian book, especially since I was deeply hurt, believing that God wasn't listening to my prayers.

After I put Meg to bed that evening, however, it was as though the book was calling out to me. Reluctantly, I fished it out of the carrot peels and soggy lettuce. Curling up in a chair with *Something More*, I never suspected that this book was about to take me on an exciting spiritual journey that would ultimately change my life in ways I could have never imagined!

As the hours passed I discovered that I was so hungry for God that I couldn't put the book down. Over the next couple of months, I bought every book that Catherine Marshall had ever written. This talented writer became my mentor, and her writing took me to a deeper spiritual level, transforming my life. I pulled out my childhood Bible, dusted off the cover, and spent hours reading the familiar verses along with Catherine's books.

Life didn't get any easier following my spiritual quest. To be truthful, it got worse, but I was different. I no longer felt hopeless ... a strange and exciting hope was welling up inside of me! Catherine Marshall had gone through tougher times than I was experiencing, so her life experiences encouraged me to rely on God as she did.

Cloud of Witnesses

Authors who are now sitting in that great cloud of heavenly witnesses can continue to be mentors in our lives through the words that they have left us. Corrie ten Boom's books have impacted millions around the world. Her ability to take the daily lessons of life and unite them with universal spiritual principles has forever changed many a person's direction in life.

My friend Georgia, just before leaving for a large women's conference, happened to read how, before Corrie ten Boom went to speak, she asked God to reveal any unconfessed sins that might block God's power.

"Lord," Georgia asked, *"Show me anything that is not allowing your spirit to flow through me."*

"Pride," is what I quietly heard in my heart.

"Pride?" I questioned. I was feeling quite humbled by life at the time. Then the Lord brought to my mind an e-mail I had quickly zipped off to a man I had dated a year earlier. I hadn't heard from him for months when I received an e-mail asking how I was doing. I promptly listed my most recent successes and achievements, that my son had been named Rookie of the Year in his college conference, and so on. Nowhere in the note did I ask how he was doing, because I was still upset with the way he had quickly terminated our relationship.

"Call him and apologize," I heard.

"Oh Lord," I moaned. But I did.

The conversation began awkwardly as I explained the reason for the call. However, soon the talk between us flowed and as I hung up the receiver I felt a huge weight lifted off my heart. It was an unbelievably healing time, and my presentations that weekend were especially powerful—just like Corrie had taught me.

Another time Corrie mentored Georgia was when she was traveling home from a weeklong series of meetings and was very tired. She made a comment to her traveling companion, who snapped back. "Georgia, it's not about you."

"Immediately," Georgia said, "I felt egotistical and hurt, and thought about how horrible I was. But then I remembered the story of Corrie being so tired when speaking in Cuba that she secretly hoped no one would come forward to accept Christ. Later she realized how awful and selfish that thought was (but she had been exhausted). Anyway, I shut up the accuser in my mind who was telling me what a terrible awful person I was. Again, Corrie had mentored me."

Life-Changing

Books not only mentor us in areas of personal or spiritual growth, they can also impact and change things that we never realized needed changing. It was that way for Eva Marie Everson when she discovered a new dimension to her prayer life through reading a book.

I've always been a pray-er. I learned "Now I lay me down to sleep" when I was but a small child. I said, "God is great," before every meal. Each Sunday school lesson was headed up with a prayer to the Lord; every sermon I sat in the hard pews and squirmed through began and ended with a prayer. I knew the Apostle's Creed (a sort of prayer) before I knew much else. I sang the Doxology (another sort of prayer) while standing between my mother's soprano and my father's bass voices.

When I aged and matured, I learned the importance of prayer. I prayed my mother would become well again. I prayed for my father during a difficult period in his career. In the sixth grade, when my teacher asked if anyone would like to give the opening day prayer, my arm was the first one that stretched toward the ceiling. "Me! Me!" I loved to pray! At the end of the year, my teacher wrote in my autograph book: "To Sweet Eva Marie, the only student in my class who isn't afraid to pray."

I understood prayer ... but I had never truly tapped into the importance ... the necessity ... the intimacy of my prayer life until I read a book by Robert Benson, *Living Prayer.* Prayer, he writes, must be *lived* ... not merely spoken, or given. One paragraph in particular touched me like no other.

"If the Christ is to be seen in this world now, then what happened to the Christ must happen to us. We who call ourselves His friends, who call ourselves His Body even, must have done to us what was done to the bread on the night that He gave it to His friends and told them what was to happen that God might be glorified. We too must be taken, blessed, broken, and shared. We must somehow stop offering ourselves *in* prayer and begin offering ourselves *as* prayer."[2]

Something inside of me stirred when I read those words. I couldn't explain it perfectly then ... and I still can't. I only know that from that moment on, I viewed my time in prayer with God as being *with* God. From the moment I first become conscious each morning, my thoughts immediately go to him. We chat all day long. Sometimes our conversations are more intense than others. Sometimes I cry. Sometimes I laugh. Sometimes I just let it all out and tell him exactly how I feel.

And he hears me. I know ... because now he talks back. He responds. He and I are living in a never-ending conversation. And I owe it all to a paragraph in a book ... and a man who was willing to write it.

Books can be a temporary safe place for learning until we are ready to share personally. There may be areas in your life where you have struggled with doubt and have not known of others with whom you have felt it was "safe" to share those doubts. I love the way God knows, understands, and brings about resolutions to those doubts in his time and way. Our niece's husband, Jeff, told me about his experience along these lines. Again, God used a book to divinely intervene in Jeff's life.

Hugh Ross is an astronomer and pastor whose book *The Creator and the Cosmos* (and other literature) has had a tremendous impact on my thinking and in my witness. My view of history and of the validity of the claims of modern science has changed dramatically in a matter of a year or so because of his ministry.

I grew up a full-fledged agnostic, which came from the mingling of my parents' atheism with my grandmother's Catholicism. Mostly, I remember the influence of watching *NOVA* and National Geographic specials with bowls of popcorn in front of us. Science was god in our house. It was good, benevolent, and, eventually, all knowing. Objective altruists digging up bones or analyzing the wonders of DNA were coming up with all the answers. One of those answers seemed to be that there is no God, and that religion is the product of unenlightened superstitious primitive men. Religion survived, it seemed, only because so many choose to remain unenlightened.

Well, despite that background, by God's will alone I still managed to become a Christian. Yet to make the change, I turned my back on almost everything to do with science.

Fortunately, there were Christian scientists who had

plausible answers to my many concerns and questions about evolution (my biggest obstacle). That alone was enough to keep my intellectual apprehensions at bay. But I still had so many other questions.

Good answers never came ... so I eventually resorted to covering my ears and humming every time someone started taking about millions or billions of years. It was frustrating because I had no meeting ground where I could share my faith with my science-oriented family or anyone else like them. My beliefs were absurd in their eyes. While they might be open to the spiritual truths, they would reject them because of their strong connection to my belief in "scientific absurdities."

I knew that there had to be something more, so in frustration I turned to books. I eventually came across Hugh Ross, a scientist with a Ph.D. in astronomy from the University of Toronto and a former research fellow at Cal Tech.

In his book *The Creator and the Cosmos* he shows how modern scientific discoveries are continually reinforcing the case for the God of the Bible. My fear was that he would prove to be a scientist who either denied the inerrancy of Scripture or came up with entirely implausible interpretations in order to accommodate his scientific views. Neither was the case! His interpretation of the creation accounts in the Bible was the most compelling I had ever read, and in subsequent studies, it continues to be so!

This has rejuvenated my interest in modern science and has given me a mission: The more I learn about science, the more I will find reasons to believe in the God of the Bible.

I know that the efforts of Hugh Ross have made a big difference in my life, and I am very thankful that God has placed his ministry in my spiritual path.

Day and Night

Many a time, when I have had a vague sense of dissatisfaction with life, I have gone to my library and just browsed through the books. I usually feel drawn to one, and if I pick it up and begin to read, I often find new insights and direction that are just what I need at that moment. A friend of mine confirmed this by sharing her recent experience.

I had several book proposals I had promised to submit, a garden that needed tending, and a list of projects that must be completed within six months. It was staggering. *"Oh, Lord,"* I poured out in my quiet time, *"I can't do this. Please help me!"*

Feeling a gentle nudge, I picked up the book *Experiencing God* from my nightstand. I opened it to where the bookmarker had been placed—page thirty-two. My eyes glanced over the page and focused where I had drawn an arrow months earlier. I couldn't believe what I read, *"God will accomplish more in six months through a people yielded to Him than we could do in sixty years without Him."*[3]

The passage used the same time frame I had been struggling with—six months. Immediately I let out a sigh of relief and remembered a comment shared by a

Christian woman: *"If you can do everything, why do you need God?"*

Good question! I love the fact that God is always faithful to remind me, when I get so caught up in the pressures of the moment, that seeing things from his perspective keeps life in the proper order.

God is so faithful to bring into our lives just what we need, right when we need it the most. Sometimes that happens through a personal contact, but God is not limited in his mysterious ways of working in our lives. Many times it can be through books. Reading about the struggles and triumphs of the men and women who have authored these books is another form of mentoring, which we can take advantage of at any time, day or night. Observing the growth, struggles, responses, and decision-making processes of those who have gone before us can provide insight, challenge, and often practical help for our own situations.

Personal Evaluation

1. What are your favorite books? Have their authors been mentors for you?
2. What unmet need for mentoring could be met by a book? Look for such a book.

CHAPTER EIGHT

Look Into God's Word

The greatest mentoring source that is available to us is the Bible. I could fill an entire book with the many different verses that God has used to change my thinking, actions, and attitudes.

Likewise, it was the words of Scripture that turned around the marriage of Yvonne and Bob Turnbull. "We were miserable," Yvonne recalls. "We didn't know how to put a marriage together. Though we were teaching God's Word, we didn't apply what the Word of God teaches."

Clashing repeatedly, the couple had reached their lowest point when God gave each of them a message of hope, as Bob tells us:

One night while I was driving home from football practice, a verse popped into my head: "May the God of hope for your marriage fill you with all joy and peace in your marriage as you trust in Him, so that you may overflow with hope for your marriage by the power of the Holy Spirit" (Rom 15:13, NIV, "Revised Turnbull Version"). I rushed in the house to share it with Yvonne, only to discover that she had just been reading that same verse a few minutes before I walked in. We both got goose bumps. It was hardly a coincidence.

"In the Bible, God promises us that life will be different if we trust in Him," Yvonne says. "We said, 'OK God, now you're *really* in charge.'"

God met them at their lowest point, giving them a reason for hope contained in his Word—Romans 15:13. Things didn't change overnight for the couple, but this encounter in the Word gave them a message that things could be different if they truly trusted in God, which they finally did.

In Armené's case, it was through immersing herself in the Scriptures that she found the peace and release she needed.

I never imagined how my life might change with one ring of the doorbell. But it did. I signed for the heavy envelope, completely unprepared for its shocking news. I was being sued, along with several others, for nearly a million dollars by a former employee of a company where I no longer worked! Pages of false accusations and twisted facts severely threatened my finances and reputation and made me feel sick.

Overwhelmed by fear, I couldn't sleep or eat. In complete panic, I murmured an incessant mantra: *How am I going to get through this?* Over the next days, I cried to anyone who would listen, especially God. Then one morning, during my devotional time, I read Queen Esther's story. I was struck that she, too, had been terrified and overwhelmed but had asked God for a practical plan to deal with her crisis. I began to ask God to give me a plan to help me get through mine.

As weeks of depositions dragged on into months, I kept opening my Bible with a new attitude of expectancy. Soon, single, workable steps and principles began to take shape. Some were simple—Scripture verses that I felt I was to pray aloud. Others were difficult—blessing the woman who "cursed" me, the one who was costing us so much money and causing so much heartache. One morning I read the passage in Ephesians about putting on armor for battle. I took each new directional Scripture and wrote it on a single index card, all of which I attached together. I carried them everywhere. I read them, prayed them, and spoke them every time I felt overwhelmed. Like stepping stones linked above rushing rapids, they bridged the two years that it took to get through my grueling ordeal. They were my lifeline, my teacher, my comfort, and my peace.

Then, suddenly, I was dismissed from the case as a defendant and retained only as a witness! Finally, as the last witness called to testify, I spoke the truth with calm confidence. The jury decided—against the accuser! But it was my confident testimony, they told the attorney, that convinced them of the truth. God had used his Word to take me across this threatening place in my life one step at a time.

In the above example it was Armené's constant and expectant reading in the Word during the months of preparation before and during the trial that eventually brought her to a place of peace and trust. She was looking for specific answers to a specific need. In the next story, she shares how God spoke to her in a very personal and surprising way, which began a healing journey within her soul.

No one was up yet at my mom's house on that spring morning, and I grabbed my Bible from the nightstand to read in the peaceful quiet of the dawn. My husband, children, and I had stopped to visit her for a few days during a family vacation. It was always stressful for me to be at Mom's. Somehow, when I was there, even though I had teenaged children of my own, I felt twelve years old again. She was of the old school of parenting—the one that held to the belief that praise made a child proud but criticism made her strong.

That had backfired with me, however, and instead of being tough, my self-esteem looked like Swiss cheese. I struggled with doubt, inadequacy, and uncertainty, and I crumpled like tissue paper when anyone blew on me. Being at my mom's always brought my doubts and idiosyncrasies into Technicolor, because nothing I did, no matter what I tried, was right. That morning we were leaving to continue our vacation, and I was glad. So far we hadn't had our usual blowup, and I hoped that, just this once, it might be avoided.

That morning I got as far as the second verse in the second chapter of the Song of Solomon when God tapped on my shoulder and said, *"Listen."*

"Just as the lily is among the thorns, so are you my child among the daughters" (NIV).

I could hear the bells and whistles ringing faintly in heaven. *"Listen,* this is *important."*

God was definitely trying to tell me something. *Isn't that nice,* I thought. *God thinks I'm OK.* I smiled, marked the date in the margin of the page, and kept on reading.

Within minutes the house was stirring and we were assembling for breakfast. But nothing went well at breakfast. I didn't eat the right things in the right amounts, I hadn't agreed with something that Mom had said, I wanted something I shouldn't have. Mom's anger intensified until she was accusing me of having done and said things the day before that had caused her to be up all night crying. She tore me to pieces in front of my children until I was sobbing and begging her forgiveness. We finally made our way to the car, where I cried for the next four hours. My younger son patted my shoulder from the backseat and said, "Mom, you were totally attacked."

I was as devastated as I had ever been. But slowly, as the intense pain settled dully into my soul, the words that I had read that morning surfaced. *"Just as the lily is among the thorns, so are you my child among the daughters."* Like salve on a gaping wound, God's words absorbed the worst of the pain and held me tight.

How wonderful my heavenly Father had been to prepare me in advance for what he knew would hurt me! How incredible that he saw me as a lily when I felt like such a thorn to everyone else.

Nice things to say, Lord, I thought, *but surely you know I'm a thorn. I always have been and always will be. Thanks for the affirmation, though. I really appreciate your faith in me.*

Then one day, almost five years later, God tapped on my soul again. *"Time's up,"* he said quite firmly. *"Today you will choose. You will either be my lily or their thorn."*

The argument was over. It was my choice. And yet, deep down, I knew it wasn't a choice at all. Because I knew that if, indeed, I called him "Lord," and he wanted me to be his lily, I had no choice. I would have to give up my old identity and take on his new name for me. In a wordless moment of fear I bowed my heart and begged him to help me. That day we began an incredible journey of divine mentoring in which he tenderly and carefully healed and built up the walls of my personality until I learned to stand as straight as a tiger lily and translucent as a calla lily. And, a funny thing happened. As I grew into my new name and identity, I was able to see that my mom's anger came from her own childhood wounds and rejection, not from my behavior. I was able to assume a maternal role with her, learning when to say a firm no, finally recognizing that her criticism had nothing at all to do with me.

As you "look up" to the witnesses who surround you, I encourage you to keep ever before you God's ultimate mentoring tool. As you immerse yourself in his Word, God will speak to your heart and lead you in his path.

Personal Evaluation

1. How has God mentored you through his Word?
2. Ask God to open your eyes to see and your ears to hear what he has to say to you in the next few weeks as you look regularly—and expectantly—into his Word.

CHAPTER NINE

Look for the Spoken Word

Mentoring can also come through words spoken by another that resonate deep within us. Sometimes those words are spoken by friends, other times by perfect strangers we may hear on the radio or on a public platform. Sometimes the words are planted in our subconscious and God brings them to mind at just the right time. At other times, God uses the words of another to lead us into a new path for our life. It was like that for Luis Palau.

During my first semester at Multnomah School of the Bible, Major Ian Thomas, founder and director of Torchbearers, the group that runs Capernwray Bible School in England, spoke at our chapel service.

Ian Thomas talked about Moses and how it took this great man forty years in the wilderness to learn that he was nothing. Then one day Moses was confronted with a burning bush—likely a dry bunch of ugly little sticks—yet Moses had to take off his shoes. Why? Because he was on holy ground and God was in the bush!

Here was Major Thomas' point: God was telling Moses, "I don't need a pretty bush or an educated bush or an eloquent bush. Any old bush will do as long as I am in the bush. If I am going to use you, it will not be you doing something for Me, but Me doing something through you."

I was that kind of bush: a worthless, useless bunch of dried-up sticks. I could do nothing for God. All my reading and studying, asking questions, and trying to model myself after others was worthless. Everything in my ministry was worthless unless God was in the bush. Only He could make something happen.

Thomas closed his message by reading Galatians 2:20 (NIV): "I have been crucified with Christ and I no longer live, but Christ lives in me." My biggest spiritual struggle was finally over! I would let God be God and let Luis Palau be dependent upon Him.

I ran back to my room and in tears prayed in my native Spanish. "The whole thing is 'not I, but Christ in me.' It's not what I'm going to do for you, but rather what you're going to do through me."

That day marked the turning point in my spiritual life. The practical working out of that discovery would be lengthy and painful, but at last the realization had come. We have everything we need when we have Jesus Christ living in us. It's His power that controls our dispositions, enables us to serve, and corrects and directs us (see Phil 2:13, NIV). I could relax and rest in Him. He was going to do the work through me.[1]

God spoke through Major Ian Thomas' words to bring a young man to his knees in recognition that great work for the kingdom can be done only through God's power, not man's.

Luis Palau has seen God work through his ministry to bring millions to salvation through Jesus Christ.

Good Advice

Georgia is single, and her friends and family are always trying to find her a mate. She struggled with knowing what God would have her to do. God sent some speakers into her life who clarified what she had already believed.

My mother, son, and several friends had said, "No wonder you don't date—you never go to any single events or dances. You don't do anything or go anywhere that you could meet a man." One person even suggested that I put an ad in the personals section of the newspaper. None of these ideas appealed to me.

I was doing a workshop at a single parent conference at Sandy Cove Christian Conference Center. John Fischer and Nancy Honeytree were the keynote speakers. As I was driving there, I was struggling with the issue of dating and meeting men. After all, I reasoned, if God had a man for me, he was all-wise and powerful and could bring him into my life—even if I do spend most of my time speaking at women's events. Yet there were also strong doubts in my mind; maybe my family and friends were right. They were my friends and family and they really cared.

In the course of the three-day conference, John and Nancy each shared their convictions that singles should focus on God's calling for their life. And in the process of following that path, God would simply have someone cross your path if it was his will for you to marry.

"*Yes!*" is what I kept whispering under my breath all weekend. That was what I believed. John and Nancy are now married (not to each other but to different people) but their lives are a testimony of what they were suggesting. Both met their spouses "on the way" of doing God's work.

What a contrast the drive home was from that retreat. I felt such a freedom to follow what I had believed in my heart was the truth.

Georgia is still single, and still trusting God while doing God's work. During the times of loneliness, or when friends and family nag her to get out and "look around," Georgia remembers the words of John and Nancy, and the promise of God to meet her needs.

Radio
There are many wonderful radio programs that reach across the airwaves, impacting lives and bringing hope to hungry hearts. God uses them in mighty ways to reach and teach people who may never think of entering a church or Christian meeting. It was the "Haven of Rest" program that did so in one man's life. His wife tells the story.

My husband was insistent. "I know that man," he whispered again, even more emphatically than the first time, as though scolding his own memory for its failure.

How could you? I wanted to reply. For, after all, we had just moved to this new place half a country away from Ohio and we knew no one. But replies had to wait. We were in the middle of a church service and "that man" was reading the Scripture passage of the day. So, in contrasting states of exasperated excitement and bewildered ignorance, we focused again on the speaker.

He was a handsome man, with a presence about him that radiated sincerity, compassion, and love. He was one of those people whom you instantly know has spent time with God. But it was his voice that captivated me. Deep and resounding, even somewhat mesmerizing, it seemed to infuse new life and authority into the passage I had heard so often. I glanced at my husband, whose smug, delighted smile now told me that he had finally remembered.

The service ended and as we spilled out of our pew and into the aisle, my husband began chattering again about the man. Now he was quizzing me. "Didn't you recognize his voice?"

"Not really."

"On the radio, remember?" he prodded.

"No, not at all." Now I was exasperated. As we closed the car doors and buckled our seat belts, I tried to bring an end to the rising tension of my not knowing and his not telling who "that man" was. Finally he took a deep breath and throttled his excited explanation down to a more understandable tempo. But never one to get quickly to the point, he started his story from the beginning.

"Maybe you aren't aware of this, but back in Ohio when my life was so out of control and I lived in panic and terror most of the time ..."

Yes, of course I remembered. How could I forget? Our whole family had been out of control and suffering badly from it. We

*had been in desperate need of God and were looking for him in
all the wrong places.*

"... I was traveling a lot then with my job but each
night, no matter where I had been or what I had been
doing, I made sure to be in my hotel room by eleven
o'clock to tune in to the radio. There was a half hour
program on then, called "Haven of Rest." The man who
hosted and narrated the program kept telling about God
and his love for me. It was my only half hour, out of every
twenty-four, completely free of panic and pain. For those
thirty minutes my thoughts seemed sane and I could
breathe. I would lie back on the pillow and absorb God's
peace and presence as it poured from that man's voice.
That man and his message became my lifeline, my assurance that God loved me and would find me.

"And now that he has, he has let me find that man.
Now I can tell him that he was on that program for me.
It was his voice that God used to tell of his love and promise. It was his message that taught me what God's light
and love are like. That man is Paul Evans."

The years passed, and as we got to know Paul Evans
and his wife, Babe, I fell in love with both of them, as did
everyone who was touched by their lives. Their love and
compassion never wavered. Their joy infected us all.

But Paul's mission in my husband's life was not over,
for healing is often an ongoing event and my husband
was still on his journey. As he continued to walk through
the ghosts and shadows of his past, Paul and Babe were
there, encouraging us, telling us with sincere love, "We
pray for you each morning."

We both got to know "that man," Paul. We will always remember him because he made an impact on our lives, both over the airwaves and in person. And he continues this very day to impact us. For now he is one of those in the cloud of witnesses. Still compassionate, still encouraging, still rooting, still saying, "There *is* rest for your soul in Christ."

God is so faithful to speak to us, through his Word and the words of others. As you read a book or listen to a radio program, your pastor, a Bible study teacher, an inspirational speaker, or to tapes, open your eyes and ears to listen for the still, small voice of God, giving you new insights, directions, corrections, and encouragement. Let God use the gifts and ministries of others to be your mentor when you most need them.

There is an old saying, "When the student is ready, the teacher appears." I like to think of God as being that teacher, but using books, tapes, speakers, or other incidents to be his messengers. Mentoring often comes in the form of truth being shared at just the right time. If we discipline ourselves to have "eyes that see and ears that hear" and to look up with expectant eyes, we will find God at work in many different ways throughout our lives.

Personal Evaluation

1. Which public speakers have been used by God to mentor you in specific ways?
2. How have those "mentoring moments" changed your life?

CHAPTER TEN

Look for Divine Intervention

Some of the most exciting mentoring experiences are those that come to us unbidden, a surprise. They are orchestrated by God, not by us. I call this divine interventional mentoring. God, knowing our need before we do, sends us messengers, sometimes in person, other times through a speaker or writer. Look for the many ways God has divinely intervened in your life. As you become aware of his working in the past, you will begin to eagerly look for and expect him to continue his work throughout your life.

"Years ago, at a time in my life when I felt no need for another best friend," JoAnne Larson told me,

I found myself sought after by a new acquaintance. In addition to socializing as couples, she would initiate weekly (sometimes more often) interactions with just the two of us and our children (usually at my house). Being a more solitary person who covets alone time, I found this somewhat of a sacrifice. She was not really an aggressive person; in fact, rather guarded and a little difficult to get to know. But I soon discovered her to be extremely intelligent, with a mature Christian experience.

When she and her husband asked us to be godparents

to their second child, we were flattered, surprised, and a little hesitant because we hadn't known them long and we realized this would tie us closely for life. Saying yes proved to be one of the best decisions ever for me. Over the years we have not only become close friends, but also she soon became a real mentor to me. She has often displayed divine direction, for example, by recommending just the book I need right *before* I need it. Because they have lived all over the world, she would sometimes show up for a week's visit—usually with all three children and often at Christmastime or other extremely inconvenient times. Even though I'm not one who relishes houseguests, her visits often proved uncannily timely—when I needed heart-to-heart prolonged discussion with someone possessing divine insight. I was therefore usually as sorry to see her go as I had been to see her come.

During the ten-plus years I led Word study groups, I sometimes found "pastoring" fifteen to twenty-five women draining, and toward spring would occasionally border on burnout. My connection with my friend was a gift from God at those times. She was *my* personal pastor, and I thank God for her!

Brief Touches

JoAnne's divine interventional mentor came into her life unexpectedly, but turned out to be a lifelong friend. Other mentors touch our lives only briefly. God has sent a series of such mentors into my life, for brief moments when I needed them most.

In 1967 my husband's employer decided to move the entire

company from Oregon to Arizona. It was very difficult for me to leave behind my entire family, the church in which I had been raised, and all our friends. The only people we knew in Arizona were other families who had also been transferred. None of them were "evangelical Christians." Most of them were Roman Catholic, and to my mind, only "religious" without any personal relationship with the Lord. I was very lonely and hungry for Christian fellowship. I don't remember why, but Fred's boss' wife invited me over. She was the younger, second wife, raising the six children left behind when his first wife died, and now she, also, had five children of her own. I don't remember how the topic came up, but she began to talk to me about the Lord. The more we talked, the more I realized she knew about the Bible. I also began to realize that she had a very close walk with the Lord, and in fact was in far closer touch with him than I. She had become part of the Roman Catholic charismatic movement and enthusiastically shared with me the power and presence of the Holy Spirit. Her enthusiasm and obvious closeness to the Lord sparked a desire in me to discover how a person whom I had considered to be only nominally religious, certainly without the benefit of an "evangelical" background like mine, could know so much more about the Scriptures, and have such a closer personal relationship with God, than I. That brief encounter with Suzanne, along with some books and tapes she suggested I might want to get, started me on a search that changed me from a judgmental, self-righteous Christian to an enthusiastic disciple of Jesus Christ.

A year later God used another Roman Catholic sister to help me fall more deeply in love with Jesus. Sister Margarita was the speaker for our new little church's first women's retreat. I was still skeptical that a nun could be theologically correct enough to teach me anything. Sister Margarita called herself a "wonderologist" and proceeded to show us by her example and stories the "wonders" of God's love. This was a woman who was so obviously in love with Jesus Christ that she figuratively took me by the hand and walked me into his arms of unconditional love. I remember one of the songs we sang, "He Touched Me," which was popular at that time. That weekend, I experienced the touch of Christ in a new way. I had received Jesus as a child, but now he was more than my Savior, he was my friend and companion. I began to understand the place of the Holy Spirit, and I had an incredible hunger to know, read, grow, and share God's love and purpose. God grabbed me at the root of my self-righteous prejudices and began to teach me that his love was not contained in any one denomination or group of people.

God's Preparation

God can also send people into our lives to get us ready for the next task he has for us. "WoWo" was an unlikely person to set someone on a whole new career, but that is exactly how God used her in Eva Marie's life.

I met WoWo when she was seventy-three years old and no bigger than a minute. The tallest she ever stood was four-foot-four-inches, and age had shortened her by three inches. She had a gentle way about her and a quick mischievous laugh ... as if she were up to something and only she knew what it was.

Though we were formally introduced in 1980, I didn't really get to know her until 1993, when she moved from her home in Atlanta, Georgia, to Orlando, Florida, where I live. By this time she was eighty-six and I was fifty years her junior. We spent a lot of time chatting on the telephone or eating ice-cream cones that I had bought from a nearby TCBY. WoWo loved ice cream.

Over the next year I drove to WoWo's about three times a week to help pass the days that were long and boring for her. When it was time for me to drive home and prepare my family's dinner, she never wanted me to leave. It was hard for me, too.

During those months an idea had been tickling my brain ... an idea for a novel. I hadn't written fiction in years, but one afternoon, when the ideas were stronger than my good sense, I went to the computer and pounded out the first chapter. The next day I read it to WoWo. When I was done she just stared at me. For a moment I thought she had fallen asleep with her eyes open.

Then she spoke. "When I was a little girl my mama used to take me to the library every week of the year. I would check out five or six books because I loved to read. And do you know what?"

"What?"

"I never once read anything from the library any better than that."

"Do you really think so?"

"I want you to promise me you'll do something with this," she said. "Do you promise me?"

"Yes, Ma'am."

"WoWo," I said later during one of my visits. "Guess what? A publisher is interested in my book!"

"I knew it," she said. "I always knew you could do it!"

"Only because of you, WoWo! If you hadn't encouraged me, I would have never written another word!"

"You're good," she said firmly. "Don't ever let anyone tell you that you aren't."

In late August 1998 I delivered the eulogy at WoWo's funeral. I spoke lovingly of a woman who encouraged me and loved me in such a way that she left me aching in the lack of her presence. I shared memories and anecdotes that brought both laughter and tears from the mourners.

When her body was finally laid to rest beneath the earth, I pulled a single pink rose from the floral blanket, brought it home, and laid it on my desk, where it dried perfectly. There it remains, close to her linen handkerchief.

I am now, professionally, a published author. Not one word would have been written had it not been for WoWo's encouraging love.

Not a moment goes by that I don't miss her!

Not a day goes by that I don't picture her, glancing over her shoulder, keeping watch at the Pearly Gates ... waiting there for me.

Life-Changing Encounters

God sometimes speaks to us in the darkest hours of life, when we are so desperate that we are willing to stop and listen to his voice. At other times God unexpectedly gives us guidance when we least expect it. It was at a simple book signing session that Charlotte Adelsperger heard God speak. She tells the story in her own words.

I heard Dr. Laubach speak a number of times when I was in my late teens. I had an opportunity to visit with him personally. Most of all, I was impressed with the spirit of Christ that emanated from him. I could just feel it and see it in his eyes! I think it came from his deep desire to practice being aware of the presence of God moment by moment. I was in awe of how he offered himself to God in reaching "the little people"—those who could not read, no matter where they lived in the world.

I shall never forget my moment with Dr. Frank Laubach in 1964. He was about to autograph for me one of his many books on prayer, when a feeling of urgency swept over me.

"Dr. Laubach," I said, taking a deep breath, "what is the most important advice you can give me as a Christian?"

He looked at me with his kind eyes, and then wrote, "We need to be saturated with Christ every day."

Hearing Dr. Laubach speak, meeting with him, and reading his books all filled me with a desire to focus on Christ's presence in my daily experiences. At times I slip back and get preoccupied with situations. One of the things I learned from Dr. Laubach that I practice often is to pray silently for those I encounter and for each one in a discussion group or any gathering. I also learned from him that focus is a "game of minutes," and when I fail, I just start over and keep trying.

What I took in from his life brought an assurance of the reality of Christ. I believe I am stronger and better equipped because of Dr. Laubach's writings, as well as his words to me that day .

I believe that God's directions for our lives are often shown through the people his providence brings into our lives. Open your eyes and begin looking for the unexpected "strangers" that God, in his loving providence, brings to you.

Personal Evaluation

1. Has God brought someone into your life unexpectedly who has set you on a new path?
2. At the time did you realize God was intervening, or did that come as hindsight?

CHAPTER ELEVEN

Situational Mentoring

A strange woman was with Cindy in the doctor's office. Someone she had never seen before. Someone she didn't necessarily want to be next to when the doctor broke the devastating news: "You have breast cancer."

"You don't remember much. You just remember that it's like somebody hitting you in the face with a baseball bat," said Cindy, who was diagnosed with breast cancer several years ago.

The doctor talked, but it was hard to hear what he said. Soon that woman, that stranger, took her hand. She translated what the doctor said. She assured Cindy that this was a beginning, not an end, and offered herself up as living proof: That woman, that stranger, was a breast-cancer survivor herself.

"She was there for my first chemotherapy, which is the scariest day of your life. We laughed, we talked, and it made chemo doable. She became a lifeline, a saving grace. I was really terrified. There would be times when I would call her, crying, I'd be so upset. And she would reassure me and say I'd be OK."

Cindy recalls how much it meant through those frightening first days to have someone who had been where she was to walk beside her and help her make sense of all that was happening.

Mentoring occurs sometimes when we are faced with a specific need. However, at that point our need may be so overwhelming that we don't know how to ask for or seek help from another. This is exactly the time that we do need to reach out and ask for help. Or, if we have already been through a particular experience, it is time for us to reach out and offer our support to someone who is now facing a similar circumstance. It was because of situations like Cindy's that St. Joseph Hospital in Orange, California, founded a mentoring program to help women and their families through the maze of fear, questions, and treatments that accompany the diagnosis of breast cancer. Survivors volunteer their time to share with women who are newly diagnosed and to shepherd them through the many decisions that lie before them.

Your need may not be as drastic as Cindy's. It may be as simple as asking for help in everyday life situations such as childrearing, home decorating, cooking, minor marriage questions, or even where to find the best bargains. The key to finding a situational mentor is to look around until you find a person who appears to have more experience than you in the area in which you desire help. Situational mentoring relationships are less deliberate, often empowering a person in very specific ways for shorter periods of time. They may not develop into ongoing relationships.

I have learned through the years that many different people can mentor us in different ways. When we were transferred to California I felt very lost and alone. New in an unfamiliar area, I wanted to furnish our home and had no idea where to find anything. To stay within my budget, I needed to be able to make my own draperies and was used to shopping in specialty discount stores. Fred inquired of people with whom he worked, and one man declared that his wife knew everything about shopping! I contacted her, and she became my "mentor" in shopping. As a matter of fact, to this day she is still my "shopping mentor." She loves shopping and stays on top of what is the latest in every area. I just want to know where to get the best deal on what I need at the moment. I don't want to spend hours and hours researching. She meets my "situational" need.

Your "situational" need may be for something very different than shopping. These days, when we are looking for answers to specific needs in our lives we are prone to sign up for classes, run to the library or bookstore, or check out the Internet to see what has been written on the subject. We may find help that way. Yet more often than not I have found that my situation is unique, not quite answered in that book or class. I want someone to talk with who will hear my concerns, for even as I talk to another I may find new insights.

I am sure when Cindy was told that her mammogram looked suspicious she began to look for books or classes to tell her what to do next. Yet the books and classes couldn't hold her hand, or sit with her through her chemotherapy sessions. Having someone beside her who had already walked the path ahead of her, to guide her along the way, helped Cindy.

Our situational mentoring arrangements do not need to be long-term involvements. Mary, the mother of Jesus, needed someone with whom to share the amazing thing that had happened to her with the appearance of an angel. Yet who would understand and believe that God had chosen her to be the mother of the Messiah? Mary immediately thought of her cousin Elizabeth. Elizabeth had also experienced a miracle, for she, who had been barren, was with child. Mary ran to Elizabeth, poured out her heart, and received the comfort and encouragement she needed. Elizabeth's support must have helped carry Mary through the many difficulties she faced being a young, unwed, pregnant Jewish girl. Nothing more is said of the relationship between Mary and Elizabeth after this time, but for the months that Mary lived with her, Elizabeth's wisdom and companionship met Mary's situational need.

"I've Been Through Things"

Each of us has some area of expertise or experience, even if it is simply gained from having lived longer and experienced things. One woman, when asked to consider what her gifts might be in helping others, pondered silently for a minute and then responded, "I've been through things."[1] Look around for those who have already "been through" the things that are facing you. Be available to others who are facing things that you have already been through. It isn't so much a matter of age bringing wisdom, but experience.

A situational mentor does not need to be someone who has all the answers to your questions. One lady described her need this way: "I am experiencing a deep trial in my life at this time. My husband is very ill with cancer. Would you know of a woman who has experienced a similar trial and would be willing to reach out to another? I am in the Word daily, and have a close relationship with the Lord. I guess what I am asking for is someone to hold my hand and tell me I am going to make it." Just finding someone who has "been through" what you are currently experiencing and is willing to listen to your hopes and fears is often enough.

Whether your need is restoring a marriage after the devastation of an affair, or knowing what to do with a drug or alcohol problem within the family, ask God to guide you to someone who has successfully navigated that path before you. A listening ear, a caring heart, and a hand to hold are often what are most needed.

Sometimes you may not find a person who can or will be a situational mentor to you. Don't give up; look for books, tapes, speakers, seminars, or classes, or search out Christian sites on the Internet. What you discover may open the doors to the answers you are seeking.

When Ann was diagnosed with cancer fifteen years ago, she knew the importance of relaxation and peace in the process of healing. "True to my nature, I wasn't experienced in the art of relaxation ... in this my situational mentor was Perky Brandt, a nurse and author of *Two-way Prayer*. Besides her book she had recorded a tape on the subject. I used her two-way prayer tape all through my treatments—what a godsend! She mentored me with the wisdom of both her speaking and writings. She was my friend, even if she wasn't there to physically hold my hand."

Another friend was diagnosed with cancer soon after she had moved across the country. She did not know anyone in the area. Friends who could not physically be with her during her surgeries and ongoing treatments provided her with excellent books on cancer healing, recovery, and testimonies of hope. Their concern and willingness to share those resources of which they were aware were tremendously helpful to her during those lonely days of isolation and fear.

I found childrearing to be an overwhelming responsibility,

and I had little confidence in my skills as a mother. I became a regular seminar and tape junkie when our girls were little, attending all the parenting classes that were offered. Dr. James Dobson, at that time, was personally teaching parenting seminars, and I never missed one when he was in our area. I also bought his tapes, for I found that I could listen to them as I washed, ironed, sewed, and cleaned house. Larry Christensen's book, *The Christian Family*, became my encyclopedia, underlined, earmarked, and read over and over again as I sought to be that "perfect" Christian mother. I never achieved that goal of perfection, but the books and tapes did help me overcome many mistakes.

Another advantage of books, seminars, and tapes is that they may bring up questions in your own mind that are not always answered in the book or seminar. These can provide a wonderful opportunity to look around and find someone in whom you have confidence to talk with about these questions. Many mentoring relationships begin with a discovery of interests in common. While you may not have the courage to approach someone and ask him or her to mentor you in marriage, childrearing, or financial or spiritual matters, you may find that initiating conversation with that person on the topic may lead to mentoring.

Counselors, Teachers, Peers

There are a number of different types of situational mentors. Among them are the counselor, the teacher, and the peer mentor.

A counselor is a person who provides advice or counsel at

crucial times. It may be a professional family therapist, a pastor, or another person trained in facilitating decision making, transition, and healing. Counselors help us to see things from a different perspective, challenge our assumptions, and bring us to deeper emotional maturity.

A teacher is a person who has more knowledge than we in a subject that we desire to learn. He or she knows what resources are needed and available, and can present that knowledge clearly, leaving us with the responsibility of integrating it into our lives.

My prayer partner relationships over the past thirty-five years have been examples of peer mentoring. Peer mentoring requires a commitment to a friendship that goes beyond the superficial. It means caring enough for each other to lay down our lives as Christ challenges us to do.

Contemporary and historical.

There are both contemporary and historical mentors. A contemporary mentor is someone who can mentor us even without a deliberate effort on his or her part. A historical mentor is someone who has passed on but can mentor us via input from biographical or autobiographical sources. There may be little or no personal interaction with either type of mentor.

In 1973 I was privileged to travel to Calcutta, India. I have never been any place like it before or since. The sights, sounds, smells, animals, traffic, and people were overwhelming. My husband and I were there with our pastor and his wife to dedicate a school that our church had helped found. During our stay in Calcutta, friends arranged for us to visit Mother Teresa and her homes for children and the dying.

Mother Teresa met us outside the home for the dying, where she had her living quarters. Just being in her presence was awe-inspiring ... I felt as if I needed to take off my shoes (although the filth of the streets quickly banished that idea from my mind). This was a person who knew God more intimately than anyone I had ever met, before or since. While we wanted to tell her how much we admired her and the work that she and her sisters were doing in that most wretched place, she would have none of it. She invited us into her living quarters, which were nothing more than an eight-by-eight-foot space, curtained off from the other sisters' beds, containing a simple twin bed, a small chest of drawers, and a little cloth rug where she knelt to pray. She cut short our questions with questions of her own. "What were we doing for Jesus? Would we join her in prayer?" Holy moments, though they were few.

It would have been easy to go away feeling guilty, inadequate, and ashamed for all that I had, and how little I was doing for Jesus. Yet Mother Teresa didn't make me feel that way at all. Instead, she inspired me that I, too, could do what she was doing: Treat every person I met, no matter what his or her circumstances in life, as if he or she were Jesus. While I have not been successful in always doing this, I have never forgotten the tiny woman with the big heart filled with the love of God, and her simple mission statement: *See everyone as Jesus and treat them as you would treat him.*

Mother Teresa has been a contemporary mentor to me. Since her death, her works and writings live on, and through them her mentoring influence on me. She is now also a historical mentor to me.

Author and speaker Karen O'Conner tells about a woman

who has served as a contemporary model to her. This woman had been praying for Karen long before they ever met, and turned out to be a real role model for Karen, as well as a mentor and friend.

When Charles and I attended church for the first time at Mount Soledad Presbyterian Church, Fran Davis, one of the elders, greeted us at the door. We introduced ourselves and she gasped, "You're Julie Sweeney's parents, aren't you?" I was stunned. How did she know my college-age daughter, I wondered? As we talked I learned that Julie, who had attended Mount Soledad on Sundays during a summer college outreach program in San Diego with Campus Crusade for Christ, had put our names in the church prayer letter—asking for prayers for our salvation. Fran was in charge of that letter, so she was very familiar with the names on the list. She told us she had been praying for us for over a year! Imagine how we felt. And imagine how she felt, to see, standing in front of her, two very visible answers to her prayers!

We nearly cried on the spot to think that the Lord had already chosen us and put our names on the heart of someone we hadn't yet met, long before we heard him speak our names.

From that point on, Fran, who lived about two blocks from our apartment, became my dear friend, Christian mentor and model, and spiritual mother. She is nearly thirty years my senior (still alive at ninety-one). Over the years of our relationship, I have watched her life and I have seen a woman of spiritual depth, peace that truly passes all understanding despite being married to a professing atheist, uncompromising kindness and understanding, and a feisty willingness to get right to the root of a problem or concern. She has spoken words of encouragement but also has pointed out areas in me that have needed healing and repentance. Yet she always has done so with respect and gentleness and the assurance that God loves me fiercely and totally, so I shouldn't be afraid to come to him with my deepest needs or darkest sins. And because she has such practical wisdom, I learned early on not to overspiritualize things, but to keep my feet firmly on the ground and my eyes on Jesus—always Jesus.

She has modeled everything she has taught me. She has been as good as her word, and her word has been rooted in God's Word.

Fran Davis is not a famous speaker or writer, just a simple woman who loves the Lord, believes in prayer, and was willing to invest her time in discipling a new believer. Mentors do not have to be famous; they just need to love the Lord and let their lives show it.

Hello, Good-bye

The following has been circulating on the Internet over the past few months. I have not been able to ascertain the author. However, I believe it fits very well within this topic of situational mentoring, so I share it for what it is worth.

When someone is in your life for a reason, it is usually to

meet a need you have expressed. He or she has come to assist you through a difficulty, to provide you with guidance and support, to aid you physically, emotionally, or spiritually. This may seem like a godsend, and it is! The person is there for the reason you need them to be. Then, without any wrongdoing on your part, or at an inconvenient time, this person will say or do something to bring the relationship to an end.

Sometimes he dies.

Sometimes she walks away or acts up and forces you to take a stand.

Then we must realize that our need has been met, our desire fulfilled, and our friend's work is done. The prayer you sent up has been answered. And now it is time to move on.

Don't grieve when a situational mentoring time comes to an end. Thank God for lessons you have learned from your mentor. Be willing to pass those lessons on to others at their points of need. You may be the answer to another's prayer for guidance.

Do ask God for wisdom and discernment as you seek a situational mentor. James 1:5 says: "If you want to know what God wants you to do, ask him, and he will gladly tell you, for he is always ready to give a bountiful supply of wisdom to all who ask him; he will not resent it" (LB).

Personal Evaluation

1. Do you currently have a specific situational mentoring need? Do you know someone who may have already walked that path?
2. What specific things have you "been through" that may be used to help others?

CHAPTER TWELVE

Intentional Mentoring

I had a dream ... but I didn't tell anyone. I wanted to make a difference in the lives of other women, just as Corrie ten Boom, Catherine Marshall, Joyce Landorf, Daisy Hepburn, Florence Littauer, Maribel Morgan, and other women speakers had made a difference in my life. I wanted to be a speaker, but I didn't have any training or credentials. I listened and watched these women as I attended the various events at which they spoke. I prayed and shared my desire with God, but never with another human until that day in 1970 when attending a conference out of state. Seated around a lunch table, we were asked to share with our tablemates what we would do if we knew we couldn't fail. I wanted to say that I would be a public speaker ... but did I dare say that aloud? Actually putting my dream into words made me feel so vulnerable. Since I figured that I would never see these people again, I decided to take the risk and said, eyes full of tears, *"I would be an inspirational speaker."*

Somehow actually saying those words out loud became the first step in the process. I began by taking small opportunities to read prayer requests before our Bible study group, making announcements, commentating fashion shows, and, gradually, speaking for Christian Women's Clubs, then teaching an adult

Sunday school class, and finally teaching Women's Bible studies in our local church.

It was another eleven years before I got any real training in speaking. Then I was invited to participate in a new ministry founded by Florence Littauer for the purpose of training Christians to become speakers and writers. I was both excited and scared as I attended CLASS (Christian Leaders, Authors, Speakers Seminar) in 1982. I hung on every word that Florence and her staff had to say that week. I began to put into practice the principles I learned. My speaking and teaching changed, and I eagerly signed up for the advanced course. I intended to learn to become a good communicator, and CLASS was full of tools to help me. By 1984 I was honored to become a member of the CLASS staff and was able to sit under Florence and Marita's teaching several times a year. I learned not only in the seminar sessions, but as Florence would share with her staff in the nightly meetings, I gleaned new insights and methods. My intentional steps in the realm of speaking had led me to Florence Littauer. She, in turn, had made a determined effort to help people like me develop our gifts and talents.

Intentional mentors are those we seek out for a specific purpose on a longer-term basis than the situational mentors discussed in the previous chapter. While Florence and I have never had a formal mentoring relationship, I have made an intentional effort through the years to glean all the wisdom and help I can from her.

If we are serious about growing and learning in any area, we need to be intentional in seeking guidance and direction. Those who are the best in their field are there because they intentionally set out to become the best. They are willing to put in the time and effort that it takes to do whatever they have set out to accomplish.

Apprentice and Master

Apprenticeship, common through the centuries until modern times, is similar to what I am calling intentional mentoring. In apprenticeship, crafts, skills, and services were learned when a younger person came alongside someone who was already working in a profession. In the days of working together, the older person taught the younger one everything about his or her profession. Similarly, in families, several generations would live together under one roof. The young girls would learn to cook, clean, have babies, and raise them by watching and working with their mothers and grandmothers. The sons would learn to farm, raise animals, build, or do whatever their fathers did. If a child wanted to learn a skill that wasn't available in his or her own family, that child would be apprenticed to someone who could teach him or her that skill.

It is the business world that has discovered the power of intentional mentoring in the twenty-first century. Men and women who want to get ahead in their careers are encouraged to find a role model, or sponsor, within their company or field. A sponsor is someone who has credibility and positional authority within an organization, network, or profession, and uses that to guide, direct, train, and open doors for the mentee, to insure his or her success in the business. As women began to move up in the corporate world it was often said, "If you don't have a mentor, you don't have a prayer." The one-on-one association with someone higher up the corporate ladder was thought to be the only way women could advance. Fortunately, that is changing today, but both women and men in the business world are still seeking the wise and supportive counsel of those who have gone ahead.

In the Christian world, the granddaddy of mentoring is Howard Hendricks, who wrote the book *As Iron Sharpens Iron*. Hendricks' father taught him: *"Son, you'll never be a great leader until you learn how to be a great follower."* So Hendricks intentionally set out to be both.

"I caught on early that the guys who went to the top were the guys who had somebody to sponsor them, somebody who vouched for them," he said. Hendricks didn't always have a written plan or strategy for finding these mentors, "but I'm sure that it was purposeful, it was intentional. I would figure out who the guy is who's got what I want, then ask, 'How can I get next to him, spend time with him?'"

During his years at Wheaton College, Hendricks spent hours with New Testament scholar Dr. Merrill Tenney. When he went on to Dallas Seminary he lived briefly with Lewis Chafer, the school's founder and first president. Later Hendricks became a protégé of Dr. John Walvoord. "I think back on it," Hendricks said of the people who impacted his life, "and it even blows my mind to this day."

Hendricks sought time with these people and found ways he could help them. When Harry Ironside, the legendary preacher and theologian, began to lose his sight late in life, Hendricks wrote out his correspondence and acted as his chauffeur.

Ministry and education were the cornerstones of

Hendricks' life, but he didn't limit himself to people from those disciplines. "By now, I was aware of a pattern," he said. "So I would always take the initiative. If I was going into a town, I'd make an appointment with a businessman or professional or a guy in ministry who I thought had something to contribute to me."[1]

Hendricks has never stopped learning, and to this day intentionally seeks out people who can teach him something. Becoming a leader like Howard Hendricks means actively looking for mentoring.

I like what D.A. Carson says in *For the Love of God:* "People do not drift toward holiness. Apart from grace-driven effort, people do not gravitate toward godliness, prayer, and obedience to Scripture, faith, and delight in the Lord. We drift toward compromise and call it tolerance; we drift toward disobedience and call it freedom; we drift toward superstition and call it faith. We cherish the indiscipline of lost self-control and call it relaxation; we slouch toward prayerlessness and delude ourselves into thinking we have escaped legalism; we slide toward godlessness and convince ourselves we have been liberated."[2]

Spiritual Directors
Spiritual growth is something that takes an intentional mindset. This is probably the most common area for seeking mentors. The oldest form of this type of intentional mentoring is through spiritual directors. The centuries-old practice of spiritual direction is making a resurgence in today's world. Centuries ago, early Christians, seeking God, went out into the

desert to think, to pray, and to live a simple life. Eventually, the people left behind visited these holy "desert fathers," who had abandoned city life for solitude, and asked for help in knowing God. They wanted to know how to pray, to get closer to God. It was from this simple beginning that the great teaching centers in European monasteries took their root. They became the places where people went to find the answer to the question, "How do I find God?"

Spiritual direction is not a teacher-disciple or student-guru relationship. It is basically about helping people pray, guiding them on their own unique paths, discovering God's plan for their lives. Gurus tend to be more autocratic and are generally interested in a dominant relationship. Teachers, on the other hand, are trying to impart specific lessons, while a spiritual director pursues a simple one-on-one personal relationship between the creature and the Creator. The essence of spiritual guidance is two people talking about God, and their experience of God in one's life. The question is: "What is God saying to me?"

Christianity Today recently ran an interview with Jeannette Bakke, who has spent fifteen years studying, receiving, and giving spiritual direction. She describes spiritual direction: "It is a discipline in which, with the help of another, you try to listen to your own heart and to God's. It is about *intention* and *attention:* [italics mine] I desire to hear God, so I am going to make space to give God my attention. I like to say that spiritual direction is discernment about discernment, as Christians are always in the process of discernment in some way. Spiritual direction gives people a place to talk out loud and confidentially about what they are thinking about already."[3]

There are two types of spiritual directors: disciplers and spiritual guides. A discipler is a more experienced follower of Jesus Christ who helps the new believer become grounded in the Scriptures. He or she imparts knowledge of the basics on how to grow in Christ. A discipler is an encourager, often a prayer warrior, who seeks to help the new believer find Christian fellowship and understand Christian disciplines such as prayer, Bible reading, worship, and lifestyle changes.

A spiritual guide is a mature follower of Christ who not only shares knowledge and skills related to deeper spirituality, but also asks questions and provides accountability and insights for a person's spiritual growth.

There are many books written on spiritual direction, something that has been relegated in modern times mostly to Roman Catholic seekers. The renewal of interest in having a spiritual guide or director has prompted a whole new genre of books and leaders in the Protestant denominations, and is often called spiritual formation.

It is helpful to read the lives and autobiographies of the saints and others to gain insights into their spiritual growth. However, spiritual direction or formation is not a do-it-yourself enterprise. While reading is a significant part of the process, it also requires talking about and exploring one's reaction to the books, the Bible, and other experiences that are central to spiritual growth.

The value of a spiritual director lies in the resources, experiences, and compassion he or she brings to the meetings. Knowing just the right psalm to suggest, a good meditative book, an inspirational saint's life to study, offering, suggesting, reflecting back—this is the director's role. The director needs to keep his or her "self" out of the way; making it transparent, not projecting, is important. Eugene Peterson, in talking about spiritual direction, says, "Responding to God is not sheer guesswork. The Christian community has acquired wisdom through the centuries that provides guidance."[4] Spiritual direction is one of the most intentional and intensive forms of mentoring.

Varieties of Spiritual Direction

Not everyone will have a spiritual director available to him or her, but that does not need to hinder our spiritual growth. As I began to speak I applied the skills and techniques learned from classes and listening to and observing other speakers. Yet when I began teaching the Bible on a weekly basis I wanted more than just skills and techniques. I wanted the Bible to come alive, to speak to the needs of my students and impact their lives in a dynamic and practical way. I wanted to know more about the Scriptures myself. I wanted to know how to understand, interpret, and explain them. I also made an amazing discovery. I was a teacher, not an evangelist. My style was inspirational, not entertaining. I began to realize that God had been preparing me for this task for many years.

I had been "mentored" in Bible teaching through my years of listening to teaching tapes by the great Bible teachers. During the 1970s and 1980s, while our daughters were still at home, I took in sewing for extra income. Since sewing was something that came easily to me, I did not have to concentrate so much on what I was doing and spent my days listening to audiotapes of Ray Stedman, Judson Cornwall, Chuck Swindoll, John Hunter, Ian Thomas, Earl Palmer, and dozens of other preachers. I attended summer Bible conferences, went to revival services, and attended retreats, seminars, Bible studies, and any event with a special speaker. I listened to Christian radio, and programs such as "Haven of Rest" every day as I ate my lunch. I belonged to tape libraries and often bought the tapes of the speakers I had heard. I bought the Bible on tape, as well as many music tapes, including worship tapes of Scriptures in song. In many ways, God had prepared me for teaching the Bible through the years I spent listening to all those teachers. To this day, nothing gives me more joy than sitting down, studying the Bible, and preparing a lesson to teach. I intentionally spent time listening to those great teachers, and they became my spiritual directors.

Because Bible teaching is so important to me, when the opportunity arose for me to attend Fuller Theological Seminary, I had to step out in faith and begin. I was very frightened, as I had not been in school for twenty-five years. I wasn't sure I could compete with all those brilliant young people, fresh out of university. Yet I knew that God was opening a door for me and my part was to walk through it in obedience. I discovered not only that I could do it, but that I loved it. Those four years were filled with the intentionality of learning all I could from some of the best professors in the world. They became my mentors in their areas of specialty. Again, not on a personal, one-to-one basis, but rather, as I watched, listened, learned, and applied their teachings to my life.

Sometimes God surprises us as we seek mentors for one thing when it turns out he has something else in mind. Judy was looking for someone with whom she could do long training runs. At a 10K run in Yuma, Arizona, she met Margaret.

Margaret, in her seventies, with a long history of alcohol abuse, broken marriages, and unhappiness, had found Christ, who had turned her life around. Margaret had decided to make up for her years of undisciplined living by becoming an Iron Man Triathlon competitor. She, too, had been praying for someone with whom she could train. During their runs of several hours, Judy began sharing with Margaret her thoughts and feelings. She had just come out of a sinful, adulterous relationship, and while she had confessed and repented she did not feel victorious.

"God sent Margaret as a concrete witness of his love. She was helpful in directing me toward Bible study, inviting me to her church, and including my husband and me in wholesome activities and Christian fellowship. We have had fun together. She has been the most important mentor in my life."

We may seek an intentional mentor for one area of our lives and find that God uses that person to minister to us in other ways. We can learn more than we ever intended if we intentionally take every opportunity God offers!

Personal Evaluation

1. Has most of the mentoring in your past been divine intervention, situational, or intentional?
2. In what areas of your life would you like to have longer term, intentional mentoring?
3. Can you think of someone who might be able to provide that for you?

CHAPTER THIRTEEN

Look Out!

Not all mentoring is a positive experience; some is downright toxic, and some mentoring experiences can prove to be more destructive than instructive. A friend, whom I will call Jackie, relayed one of the worst to me.

I met my mentor at a Christian conference. That gave me a false sense of protection. I was in a very vulnerable place in my life, a sitting duck for someone like Gayla. She made me feel special, unique, and accepted.

We talked by phone on several occasions that year, until finally I went to visit her at her home in another state. Staying in a hotel, I went to her home daily for "therapy."

She had very different ideas about counseling, not following any conventional rules. Therapy was to be exclusively with her. She was not licensed, and claimed a license was not necessary; God had given her a special gift. She claimed an exclusive and special connection to God. One of her favorite sayings was: "I'll hold your hand and God's, until the time I can bring your hands together." The "therapy" sessions went on for hours at a time, sometimes all day. I became enmeshed with her family and other "clients." There were no boundaries. I was required to terminate contact with my parents and family of origin for at least six months in order to continue "therapy." Always I was told, "If you want to get well, you have to do exactly as I say." I was encouraged to question my previously held values and everything but what was going on in "our special relationship."

Any time a mentor or mentoring relationship becomes the focus of your life to the exclusion of all else, it is toxic and unhealthy. Yet I didn't know that then. I thought I had found someone who really cared for me and would listen to me and help me. I got caught on several fronts. First, it was the hope of finally belonging. Gayla promised connection, first with herself and then through her to God. Gayla also promoted trust, something that was foreign to me. I trusted her explicitly, though I am still not sure why. Everything was spiritualized as being connected to prayer and a "relationship" to God.

When I finally returned home I was unable to work, as I could not concentrate or function. I returned for a full month of "therapy" in 1990. After I returned home a second time, Gayla directed regressive therapy in our weekly two-hour phone sessions, and prompted through it her version of my past. Out of that a story of sexual abuse by a grandfather, father, and brother developed, totally alienating my family of origin. It never felt right to me, but Gayla had my complete, unquestioned trust. I could not trust my own reality. Therapy had rewritten the past.

In late 1990 the relationship started to come apart, as I started questioning both Gayla and myself. She told me

I was not trying to get well, and began accusing me of lying. The last time I saw Gayla was in 1991, though we continued our weekly telephone sessions until the end of that year. Gayla then told me that she would no longer see or take any phone calls from me, and that any letters I wrote would be returned unopened.

I was totally devastated. I had risked trusting someone for the first time in my life. I felt betrayed beyond belief. I was alienated from family and friends. Now I even doubted God, prayer, and Christianity, because she claimed that God had orchestrated and directed all that had gone on.

It has been a very long and hard road back to finding God and myself. Some relationships have never been restored. Others were left with scars that will never go away. My life will never be the same. Slowly, in small steps, over the last ten years, I have found healing in some of these lost relationships. God, in his graciousness and love, is also bringing me back to faith and trust in him.

Jackie had one of the most destructive "mentoring" relationships possible. As you read her story you may ask, "Why on earth would anyone allow herself to be so controlled by another?" Jackie herself now realizes that she probably did need counseling to overcome many childhood hurts and feelings of inferiority and insecurity. However, Jackie's neediness blinded her to the unhealthy aspects of her relationship with Gayla, whose needs were just as great as Jackie's, though different.

Not all toxic mentoring relationships will be as overt as Jackie's. Some will be much more subtle. Yet they can be just as destructive.

Sharene had gone to church all of her life, but just recently she had been introduced to a dynamic new church in her community. It was alive and exciting, and through the ministry of the women's Bible study, taught by the pastor's wife, Sharene had entered into a personal relationship with Jesus Christ. In her excitement, she began to volunteer for any assignment Mary, the pastor's wife, offered. Mary was thrilled to have such an eager new volunteer and began using Sharene's willingness and skills continually. As time went on, the more Sharene did for Mary and "the Lord," the more Mary expected.

Soon, Sharene's family began to resent all the time and money that she was spending on and with Mary. They began to put pressure on Sharene to set limits to what she was doing "for the Lord." The more pressure Sharene's family put on her to limit her time and involvement with Mary, the more Mary inferred that Sharene wasn't pleasing the Lord. Sharene's enthusiasm and love for the Lord was being slowly drained away. She began to doubt herself, Mary, and her faith in God. What had happened to the loving God she had met just a year or so before?

As she watched her family's resentment grow, Sharene finally shared her frustration with another mature Christian in her Bible study. Lois had been through a similar experience with Mary and had watched Mary use other new and enthusiastic Christians until she had driven many away. Lois encouraged Sharene to either put a stop to her relationship with Mary, or, if she could not do that, leave that church and find another where she could grow and mature in her faith without someone taking advantage of her gifts and skills. Unfortunately,

Sharene did eventually have to leave that church. Yet she did not give up on Jesus. She found another fellowship, which took her under its wings and gave her the nurture she needed to mature in Christ.

New Christians are often very eager to learn and don't always have the experience or discernment to "rightly divide the Word of Truth" (2 Tm 2:15, KJV). This is the experience of the writer of the next true story.

It was in the mid-seventies that God intercepted me and offered me his cloak of salvation. Oh, how I needed it! My marriage was falling apart, my husband's rages had turned to shoving and pushing, and with two small children and no job, I had nowhere else to turn. Shortly after I sobbed my complete helplessness to Christ, God moved us to a small Midwestern farm community and quickly networked me into an intimate weekly Bible study group sponsored by a women's outreach organization. A wonderful woman named Paula who had been a Christian for twenty-five years taught it. I was more than eager to learn all I could about my "new love," Jesus Christ. Like a sponge, I absorbed everything that was said, especially by Paula. She knew the Scriptures, she practiced her faith, and she had an intimate relationship with God that I wanted, too.

It wasn't long before our group broke into prayer partnerships and I, flattered beyond belief, was asked by Paula to be her partner. She said she saw spiritual depth in me and felt she could learn from me. Who wouldn't have been flattered? We met weekly for prayer and lunch. It was in those weekly meetings that I "sat at her knee," so to speak, and learned how to have an intimate relationship with God, how to pray, and how to study the Scriptures. I wanted more than anything else to please God, not out of fear, but out of incredible gratitude and love.

While my spiritual life was reviving me, my personal life was deteriorating rapidly, despite the fact that my husband had also become a Christian. It was obvious that he was very emotionally disturbed; my dilemma grew exponentially with his increasingly abusive behavior and my own spiritual growth. I didn't know what to do: Should I leave the relationship, as my deepest gut pleaded? Or should I stick it out in obedience? What would God want? I went to Paula. She would know.

Methodically she pointed out Scriptures that commanded me not only to respect my husband, but also to submit and defer to him. I was stunned that God would want me to do this but there it was, as clear as black and white, in his Word. It seemed that everywhere I turned I was hearing this message—from my church, from tapes, from national speakers. So, naturally assuming that total submission was God's perfect plan, I stopped defending myself, gritted my teeth, and deferred to every whim and wish that my husband voiced. It wasn't long before any semblance of power balance in our relationship was gone, and with his newly found power, my husband escalated his rage and abuse whenever there was any hint that he would not get his way. I continued to submit, taking to heart Paula's teaching that, through this trial, God was perfecting me, teaching me his ways, refining my heart. My self-image eroded quickly until I was convinced that I was so very impure it would take a lifetime for God to ever heal my marriage and me.

This mentoring—and the fact that I accepted it—caused enormous damage. My eagerness to please God had made me vulnerable to narrowly focused teachings that, as I learned much later, were not models of God's balance. Yes, they were from Scripture, but Scripture also showed a God who railed at injustice, as well as a God who found value in me, despite my "impurities," and who would not cleanse me of them by beating them out of me.

After three years, God moved us two thousand miles from this small Midwestern town to a place where these teachings were framed in a more balanced light. I began a long journey, with new mentors, sorting out what I had learned about what God really wanted for our family and me.

I do not harbor any malice toward Paula as a mentor, because it was she, after all, who taught me to seek God, and it was through seeking him that I found his balance. Paula has, herself, continued to grow, and now acknowledges that this teaching was destructive to many abused women.

In the years that have gone by since all of this, I have tried to remember what I've learned as God has brought women to me for counsel and advice. I've learned that, as I take to God any advice or counsel I receive from a mentor, he will take its truth and apply it personally to my life. I've learned, too, to be reticent of teachings that seem faddish. As a mentor, while I might believe something very strongly, I should offer only wisdom, not direction. God himself will show those being mentored what he wants them to do.

It is always wise to take any advice you are given and compare it with the whole of Scripture, as well as to submit it to God and ask for his clear direction on the subject. James 1:5 instructs us: "If you want to know what God wants you to do, ask him, and he will gladly tell you, for he is always ready to give a bountiful supply of wisdom to all who ask him, he will not resent it" (LB).

There are many self-help books, motivational audio and videotapes, and websites that are full of advice. We must be very discerning in deciding which of these we read or listen to. Because they may contain nuggets of truth, it is easy to become captivated by false premises or principles and find ourselves slipping, unconsciously, away from God's truth. Another often overlooked but subtler arena in which we find negative mentoring is the media, specifically television and films. Because we tend to ingest the subtleties of poor guidance into our spirits, we should be very choosy as to which programs or movies we watch.

Avoiding Toxic Mentoring

To avoid toxic mentoring experiences, ask yourself some questions.

The first thing you must ask is *"Who is this potential mentor?"* Simply looking first at the mentor as a person is sometimes the most obvious guidance you will receive. Scripture tells us that we will "know them by their fruits" (Mt 7:16, NKJV). Look at how this person leads his or her life. A good mentor will not teach one thing and live another. If you have not had the opportunity to observe someone over time, ask others who know that person well about his or her reputation. Look for signs of dysfunction, unhealthy mental or emotional patterns, or poor self-esteem. These roots might color a mentor's advice or "teaching." Do not be swayed by fame; God certainly isn't! Look at the values and beliefs this person holds. Learn about his or her role in the body of Christ, and history of keeping confidences. Does this person criticize or edify others? Do not hesitate to ask a potential mentor to tell you about what brought him or her to the Lord and what his or her life's vision—or mission—might be. Listen closely to whether this person feels he or she has a "special connection to God" or claims to have a "special" gift of healing, insight, or direction. Do not feel as though you are asking too much by wanting to know these things. After all, you are planning to entrust yourself to this person for spiritual guidance!

Then ask yourself, *"How does the mentor relate to me and others?"* We must always remember that Christ came to bring abundant life to each of us individually and that when he ascended to heaven, he left the Holy Spirit for each of us so that his Spirit could lead us personally. This means that we can each hear from God. A good mentor will help us as we seek God, often confirming his direction or confronting us when we are getting off track. Yet God will never leave our direction wholly to a single person. He desires to lead us himself in a close personal relationship.

Thus, we must be wary of mentors who want to control our

relationship with God or speak for him. Watch for subtly controlling language and behavior in a mentor. A good mentor will say, "I wonder if God is wanting you to ..." leaving you to seek him for confirmation. A controlling or directive mentor will borrow spiritual power and credibility by saying, "God has shown me that you are to..." This type of message will at the very least cause you to pause, for who would argue with God? It will certainly undermine your own confidence in hearing from God. Remember that God *does* speak to you and will confirm whether this is truly his message. You can respond to this type of control or direction by saying, "Thank you! Let me take that to the Lord and see what he will tell me." Be cautious of anyone who wants exclusive control or involvement in your life, who reacts negatively to your seeking others for advice, or who uses guilt to keep you in relationship with him or her.

Look at the way your mentor responds to your questions. A good mentor will not claim to have all the answers and will be quick to say, "I don't know but I'll pray with you about this." Look at the way in which your mentor reacts to your decisions or suggestions. Does he or she assume the role of critical parent, holding you ransom to his or her approval or responding to you in anger when you don't follow advice? Does your mentor have a critical attitude toward everyone else, making you feel fortunate for being "the only one" who is spiritual enough to understand his or her brand of truth? A good mentor will be excited and supportive as you grow, even to the point of letting go when you don't need him or her anymore. This is a sure sign that your mentor understands that his or her role is to help you lean on God, not him or her.

Looking at the relationships that your mentor has developed, whether vertical (with God) or horizontal (with others), will give you a good idea of who this person is and how he or she relates. However, it's always good to remember that your mentor is also on a growth journey and, while he or she may not be perfect, this person should be open to your positive suggestions and honest feedback about what you need.

One important way to protect yourself is to choose a mentor of the same gender so that you will not find yourself in a spiritually intimate relationship that could tempt your flesh. You will also need to keep the relationship in perspective, realizing that hearing from God and responding to his direction and opportunities is your responsibility. You will need to be sure that you have not shifted your dependence on him to an unhealthy dependence on your mentor.

Ultimately, God will develop your maturity as he uses a variety of mentors in your life. As you progress through your life, seek God's counsel in every decision. He will lead you and he will protect you.

Personal Evaluation

1. Is your prospective mentor mentally and emotionally healthy and secure? Are his or her values and beliefs consistent with yours? Is he or she trustworthy?
2. Do you feel as though you are working for your mentor's approval, or that you can't ever quite measure up to his or her expectations?
3. Is your mentor excited and supportive about your growth, even as you need him or her less and less?

CHAPTER FOURTEEN

Look Forward

The well-seasoned woman mentors and blesses all who touch her life. Now in full bloom, she is prepared to hand down spiritual heirlooms and to pass the torch to future generations.

Ann Platz

There once was a wise woman who was traveling in the mountains. One day she discovered a very precious stone in the middle of a stream. The very next day she met another traveler.

"I am very hungry," he said. "Would you have anything to eat?"

The wise woman opened her bag to share her food with him. The hungry traveler spied the precious stone in her bag. Knowing its great worth, he asked the woman, "May I have that stone?"

"Certainly," she replied, and gave it to him without hesitation.

The traveler left, rejoicing in his great fortune. He knew the stone was worth enough to give him security for a lifetime. As he pondered what a great gift the wise woman had given him, he began to realize that she still had an even greater gift. So, a few days later, he came back to the wise woman.

"I've been thinking," he said. "I know how valuable this stone is, but I give it back to you in the hope that you will give me something even more precious. Give me what you have within you that enabled you to give me this stone in the first place."

Sometimes it is not the material wealth that you possess, but rather what you have inside you, that others need. As we have journeyed together through this book we have discovered the value of having a mentor in our lives. The even greater blessing is to be willing to share the lessons we have learned from our own experiences, passing them on to others. We need to open our eyes and look forward, willing to become a mentor in the lives of others.

In the New Testament, Paul urged Timothy to pass on "the things that you have heard from me" to faithful learners who would, in turn, be able to pass them on to others (2 Tm 2:2, NIV). Ecclesiastes 11:1 advises us to "Give generously, for your gifts will return to you later" (LB).

Moses told the Israelites before they entered the Promised Land that they had a responsibility to teach their children and grandchildren what they had seen, heard, and experienced on the way there (see Dt 4:9-10, NIV). He also gave a number of suggestions for teaching God's ways to young people (see Dt 6:7-9, NIV). Proverbs 2 describes a home environment in which parents give their children valuable gifts such as wisdom, self-appreciation, understanding, and humility.

A wise rabbi once said, "There are two things humans do in life: We achieve, and we connect. Right now, everybody's achieving and nobody's connecting."[1]

Mentoring is taking the skills and expertise that we have

achieved and using them to *connect* with others, with whom we can then share what we have learned. Vicki is a mother whose children have grown, but God connected her with a young woman who needed to learn mothering skills.

Once a year Vicki and her husband volunteer as counselors for a week at a camp for foster children sponsored by her church through Royal Family Kids Camps.

Imagine her surprise one morning as she opened the daily newspaper and saw a picture of one of her husband's campers. Accompanying the picture was the story of Amy, the youngest foster mom in Orange County, California. Amy was one of eight children by the same mother and different fathers. Her life had been spent living in cars, on the streets, or in cheap motels. Yet, in the ninth grade a teacher had noted Amy's potential, and by the time Amy had graduated from high school she had both an academic and a track scholarship to UCLA. Three weeks before she was to enter school, however, a social worker had called Amy to tell her she was removing her brothers from her mother's care and that they were going into the foster system.

Amy, herself a victim of the system, had refused to let that happen and with determination and guts had convinced the social worker and the system that she could take care of her brothers. Amy was seventeen at the time.

Now, six years later, Amy was being honored as the youngest foster mother in the system, and foster mother of the year. She had kept the family together, tutoring the three boys every night. (They were a handful, learning-disabled drug babies.) She worked part-time and performed all the household duties of any full-time mother.

As Vicki read about Amy her heart went out to her and she
wanted to help. She thought perhaps she could make a difference in their Christmas, and set out to do so. Vicki got
involved and gathered people to help, but in the process she
fell in love with Amy and her boys. Vicki has come alongside
Amy, helping in practical ways, doing little things that any of
us could do if we would: shopping for household basics, buy-
ing clothes for the boys and Amy, and accompanying Amy to
court to battle for continued custody of her brothers. Vicki is
there for Amy, to be a compassionate listener and encourager,
a surrogate mother to a motherless child who has been given
the responsibility of mothering others. Vicki had no inten-
tions of becoming a mentor for Amy, but her willingness to listen to the Lord and get involved in a young woman's life has
been a life-changing experience. It wasn't Vicki's special skills
that made her a great mentor; it was her willingness to get
involved.

It is my prayer, once you have finished reading this book,
that you will not only look at all those who have already been
mentors in your life and seek new mentors for your specific
needs, but also then reach out and share the lessons you have
learned with others. *Achieving* the skills you need and then *connecting* with others to share the riches and wisdom that have
been passed down to you are what mentoring is all about.

Your mentoring of others might not be a formal arrangement. It may start out by another watching you and then coming to you for counsel. If you are living your life in such a way
that others can see God in you, Richard Swenson says, "You
will not have to search for someone to mentor. At the right
time and the right place, God will send him or her. You will

recognize them when they come to you; you will be recognized when you bring to them your wisdom, tempered with love. You will give and receive, share the lessons you have learned and in doing so, learn of the obstacles others have struggled to overcome."[2] Mentoring is an ongoing learning experience that both gives and receives. It gives us the opportunity to learn new skills and competency, as well as pass them on to others.

E-Mentoring

You may discover innovative ways to mentor, especially in the Internet age. IBM has begun such a project in the schools of Durham and Wake County, North Carolina, as reported in the Raleigh *News & Observer*.

In a world where one's time is consumed by work and family responsibilities, not everyone can spend an hour a week at a school mentoring a student. The answer to the dilemma of how to be both a good employee and a good citizen is increasingly becoming e-mentoring.

Through the use of e-mail, mentors are able to help with schoolwork, provide career advice, and resolve personal problems by being another caring adult to whom a student can turn.

"E-mentoring allows more frequency and communications," said Nicole Pride, coordinator of an IBM program in ten middle schools and one high school. "It allows IBM-ers to volunteer and make a difference and not interfere with their jobs."[3]

E-mentoring is becoming an acceptable and viable route to gain almost instant access to the help one needs. Not only is it a good place for students to learn, it can also be a wonderful place for those in older generations who are not computer savvy to get the instructions and help they need.

Your opportunities to share the wisdom and knowledge you have gained in life are limited only by your willingness to invest your time and effort in looking forward and finding those whom you can mentor. The greatest good we can do for others is not just to share our riches with them but also to reveal to them the riches they possess inside themselves. Look forward and begin to discover the riches that God has placed within you and all those around you.

Personal Evaluation

1. Who might benefit from your knowledge and experience?
2. What steps will you take to begin sharing?

CHAPTER FIFTEEN

Look In

There once was a little boy who was having a great time playing in the mud when his mother called him into the house for lunch. She waited and waited, and when he did not come, she looked out the door to discover that he was lying in the mud with his arms and legs flailing away. He was not hurt, but was not making any effort to get up.

"James, what are you doing? Why didn't you come when I called you?" she asked.

"Mother," he replied, "I am praying to God to get me up but he ain't done it yet!"

Well, James soon learned that what he was able to do himself he was expected to do. So it is with us. This book is full of examples and suggestions for how you might find the guidance you need. Yet what you do with this information is going to be up to you. God supplies opportunities for us, but he doesn't make us recognize or take advantage of them. There are several biblical examples of this.

When Peter was imprisoned, God stepped in and broke his chains, but Peter had to get up and walk out of the prison (see Acts 12:5-11, NIV). It was the same for Paul and Silas when they were imprisoned in Philippi (see Acts 16:22-40, NIV). When Lazarus was raised from the grave, Jesus instructed the bystanders to do what they could and remove the stone, and then he did what only he could do, raise the dead (see Jn 11:38-44, NIV). Jesus also requires that we participate in our growth to the extent of our ability. In the fifteenth chapter of John, Jesus instructs: "Abide in Me, and I will abide in you." He goes on to tell us that we must concentrate on believing and obeying him. If we do that, we are promised his presence, no matter what else may happen to us. The initial responsibility is ours. It has been said, "The courage to begin always separates dreamers from achievers."

I believe you have read this book because there is within you a hunger for growth. Often the best way to obtain that growth is to actively look back, around, up, and forward to the mentors God has placed in your life, past and present, and to look in to see what God might see within you.

Os Hillman said, "Few men or women of God have become extraordinary people of faith without the influence of mentors. Elijah mentored Elisha. Elisha became one of the greatest prophets in the entire Bible. One of the primary reasons for this was Elisha's hunger. Elisha wanted a double portion of Elijah's spirit. It was this hunger that drove Elisha to be sold out to God's purposes for his life."[1]

I encourage you to seek a "double portion" of the positive attributes of your mentors. I also encourage you to seek out help throughout life in all the various places you need it. In an age of independence we have a tendency to go it on our own. However, like a rock climber attempting to scale Half Dome Mountain in Yosemite National Park, we are likely to fall if we are not securely tethered to another. Ecclesiastes 4:9-10, 12 gives us this advice: "Two can accomplish more than twice as much as one, for the results can be much better. If one falls, the other pulls him up; but if a man falls when he is alone, he's in trouble. And one standing alone can be attacked and defeated, but two can stand back-to-back and conquer; three is even better, for a triple-braided cord is not easily broken" (LB).

Every day on our climb through life we have opportunities to meet or read about a "climber" who, with Christ, can become part of our rope. We also have opportunities to worship the heroes of the world, who will never pull us upward because the Holy Spirit does not guide them. Some may even become dead weights on the end of our ropes. Who will you cultivate—those who hold your rope and pull you up, or those who would drag you down? Those you admire—friends, heroes, saints, and influencers—are not accidents. You choose whom you will emulate.

Christians never climb alone. Hebrews 12:1 states that there is a cloud of witnesses at the top of the mountain cheering us on. We have read about many of these throughout this book. They are those who have gone ahead of us or those still on earth who pray for us, care for us, support us, challenge us, and mentor us. These are the ones who hold our rope, who reach out to pull us forward. It is a long climb, and we need each other. Yet, with Christ, we have the assurance that "a triple-braided cord is not easily broken."

Look around, look back, look up, look forward, and look in; as you begin to find the mentors all around you, you will not climb alone.

Notes

ONE
Who Will Mentor Me?

1. Howard G. & William D. Hendricks, *As Iron Sharpens Iron* (Chicago: Moody, 1995), 165.

TWO
Mentoring: A New Look

1. Leonard Sweet, *A Cup of Coffee at the Soulcafe,* (Nashville, Tenn.: Broadman & Holman, 1998), 180.
2. Mary Ann Rademacher Hershey, seen on a poster.

THREE
Look Around

1. Dan S. Begley, *Care Capsule,* vol. 1, #3, (Garden Grove, Calif.: Crystal Cathedral), August 1999.

FIVE
Look Back

1. Caron Loveless, *Words That Inspired Dreams* (West Monroe, La.: Howard, 2000), 46.

SEVEN
Look Into Books

1. Leonard LeSourd, ed., *The Best of Catherine Marshall* (New York: Avon, 1995), 275-76.
2. Robert Benson, *Living Prayer* (New York: Penguin Putnam, 1999), 40.
3. Henry Blackaby and Claude King, *Experiencing God* (Nashville, Tenn.: Broadman & Holman, 1990), 32.

NINE
Look for the Spoken Word

1. Luis Palau, "How I Keep Growing," *Discipleship Journal,* (Issue 118, 2000), 47.

ELEVEN
Situational Mentoring

1. Marilyn Chandler McEntyre, "I've Been Through Things," *Christianity Today,* September 4, 2000, 111.

TWELVE
Intentional Mentoring

1. Stephen Caldwell, *Sharpened Iron*, Life@Work Journal, September, 1998, Escondido, Calif., 14.
2. D.A. Carson, *For the Love of God*, quoted in *"Reflections,"* *Christianity Today*, July 10, 2000, 45.
3. Jeannette Bakke, "Making Space for God," *Christianity Today*, April 23, 2001, 88, interview by Jennifer H. Disney.
4. Bakke, 89.

FOURTEEN
Look Forward

1. Richard Swenson, interview, Life@Work Journal, July/August 1999, Escondido, Calif., 34.
2. Swenson, 166.
3. Keung T. Hui, "Is There a Mentor on the Mouse?": *News & Observer*, May 21, 2001, 1B.

FIFTEEN
Look In

1. Os Hillman, "A Man Who Has God's Favor," Internet Devotions, www.myinjesus.com, February 23, 2001.